FROM XBASE TO WINDOWS:

CROSSING OVER TO WINDOWS PROGRAMMING

JOSEPH BOOTH

M&T Books
A Division of MIS:Press, Inc.
A Subsidiary of Henry Holt and Company, Inc.
115 West 18th Street
New York, New York 10011

Printed in the United States of America

ISBN: 1-55851-480-5

10 9 8 7 6 5 4 3 2 1

Associate Publisher: Paul Farrell
Editor: Judy Brief
Production Editor: Maya Riddick
Copy Edit Manager: Shari Chappell
Managing Editor: Cary Sullivan
Technical Editors: Ceci Smith & Brian McAuliffe
Copy Editor: Michael Hughes

Dedication

To my little buddy and budette, and my wife, Sandy

Acknowledgments

I'd like to thank the whole team who made this book possible:

Judy Brief, my editor at M&T Books; Ceci Smith and Brian McAuliffe, the technical editors for this project, and Joe McPartland and Maya Riddick, Production Editors at M&T Books.

CONTENTS

CHAPTER 1:
FROM THE TOP, DESIGNING YOUR MENU

You've been writing DOS applications for years, but you need to start programming in Windows. You know Windows programming is something you've got to learn, but every time you open a Delphi or Visual Basic manual, you enter a strange realm of event loops, messages, forms, controls, and so on. The first thing you see is the need to create a form with a variety of controls. As you read on, you get a feeling of confusion, and then you see those classic lines, "If you've programmed in DOS, you need to forget everything you've learned!" or "If you don't have DOS programming experience, this will be much easier."

Well, I say, "Hogwash!" If I am told that I have to "unlearn" all the good programming habits I've learned over the years, then I am going to be somewhat leery of using Windows programs.

The purpose of this book is very simple: to get you up and running in Delphi or Visual Basic by leveraging your DOS knowledge, not abandoning it. To do this, we will develop an application using Delphi and Visual Basic in the same way we might use Clipper or FoxPro to develop a DOS application. As we work through the application, we will gradually move away from the modal, one-step-at-a-time world of DOS into the somewhat chaotic, modeless world of Windows.

Writing a DOS Application

When you plan a DOS application, one of the first things you think about is the menu structure that you need to put together for your users. We've learned this as part of top-down design, and it serves as a nice organizer for the variety of screens our system needs. The menu can be a simple affair with five to six menu options, each of which calls a program, or a nested structure where menus lead to other menus that eventually lead to the entry screens and reports. Let's begin by describing our DOS application and the menu system used to access it.

In this book, we will create an accounting system consisting of a general ledger, a checkbook, and accounts receivable/invoicing. The system is geared toward small service-oriented companies that pay bills directly from the checkbook and only bill for services rendered. There is no inventory or sales tax issues to deal with. Payroll is handled by an outside provider, so other than writing the payroll check to the provider, there are no payroll tax complexities to deal with.

To create such a system, we would first meet with our users and flush out the details. If we are very lucky, we might even get a requirements definition document or system specification. After meeting with the users and reviewing their needs, we come up with the menu structure in Table 1.1.

Table 1.1 Menu Structure

General Ledger

Chart of Accounts

Journal Entries

Post Entries

Close the Books

Financial Reporting

- Balance Sheet
- Income Statement
- Statement of Changes in Financial Position

Checkbook

Check Register

Pay Bills

Print Checks

Make Deposits

Bank Reconciliation

Accounts Receivable/Invoicing

Customer File Maintenance

Invoicing for Services

Applying Payments

Past Due Processing

Printing Invoices

Using Xbase pseudo code, the code structure in Listing 1.1 might be implemented to create this menu.

Listing 1.1 Sample menu system.

```
private nToDo,nSubmenu,nReport
clear screen
nToDo    = 1
nSubMenu = 1
nReport  = 1

do while nToDo <> 0
     @ 2,2 prompt "General Ledger"
     @ 3,2 prompt "Checkbook"
     @ 4,2 prompt "Accounts Receivable/Invoicing"
     menu to nToDo
     ***********************************************
     * Display the submenu based upon menu selection *
     ***********************************************
     do case
     case nToDo = 1     && General ledger

    @ 3,20 prompt "Chart of Accounts
    @ 4,20 prompt "Journal Entries"
    @ 5,20 prompt "Post Entries"
    @ 6,20 prompt "Close the books"
    @ 7,20 prompt "Financial Reporting"
    menu to nSubMenu

           if nSubMenu = 5
                @ 8,35 prompt "Balance Sheet"
                @ 9,35 prompt "Income Statement"
                @10,35 prompt "Statement of Changes"
                menu to nReport
           endif

    nToDo = 10 + nSubMenu       && Assign unique menu #
```

```
case nToDo = 2      && Check book

   @ 4,20 prompt "Check Register"
   @ 5,20 prompt "Pay Bills"
   @ 6,20 prompt "Print Checks"
   @ 7,20 prompt "Make Deposits"
   @ 8,20 prompt "Bank Reconciliation"
   menu to nSubMenu

   nToDo = 20 + nSubMenu      && Assign unique number
case nToDo = 3      && Accounts receivable/invoicing

   @ 5,20 prompt "Customer file maintenance"
   @ 6,20 prompt "Invoicing for services"
   @ 7,20 prompt "Applying payments"
   @ 8,20 prompt "Past due processing"
   @ 9,20 prompt "Printing invoices"
   menu to nSubMenu

   nToDo = 30 +nSubMenu       && Assign unique number
endcase

    *************************************************
    * Now process the appropriate function based on *
    * value in nToDo variable                       *
    *************************************************
do case
case nToDo = 11          // Ledger + chart of accounts
  Do UpdChart()
case nToDo = 12          // Ledger + journal entries
  Do Journal()
case nToDo = 13
       ****************************
       * and so on, ad infinitum  *
       ****************************
```

```
    endcase
  enddo
  return
```

Admittedly, this code would need additional user interface work, such as drawing boxes around the menu and saving the screen between menu calls. However, this code—or some variation of it—could be written to handle our menu system. It is orderly and tidy; the user picks a menu option, the code adjusts the number and then performs the indicated function.

Preparing for Windows

To run this menu system under Windows, we have to make some variations. Menus in Windows are based on the CUA (Common User Access) model developed by IBM. For menus, the model consists of a top menu bar with drop down choices below it. As a general rule of thumb, the options on the top bar should be short text entries. So the first adjustment we need to make is to use shorter main menu prompts. Accordingly, we will change the menu prompts from their descriptive prompts to something a little more cryptic.

DOS Prompt	Windows Version
General Ledger	Ledger
Checkbook	Checkbook
Accounts Receivable/Invoicing	Accts Rec.

There is a lot more to CUA than shortening menu prompts. The CUA model is meant to provide a consistent interface to applications. It allows *users* to quickly learn a new program because CUA programs have a consistent look and feel. We will discuss CUA in more detail in Chapter 3. In the meantime, try to make sure any applications you develop in Windows have the same look and feel as other Windows programs.

That's about it.... With these minor changes, we can put this menu structure into a Windows platform.

Starting in Delphi

When you first start Delphi's IDE (Integrated Development Environment), you see a pull-down menu (very CUA-ish) across the top and some icons below it. This is the Delphi *control bar* or main menu (see Figure 1.1).

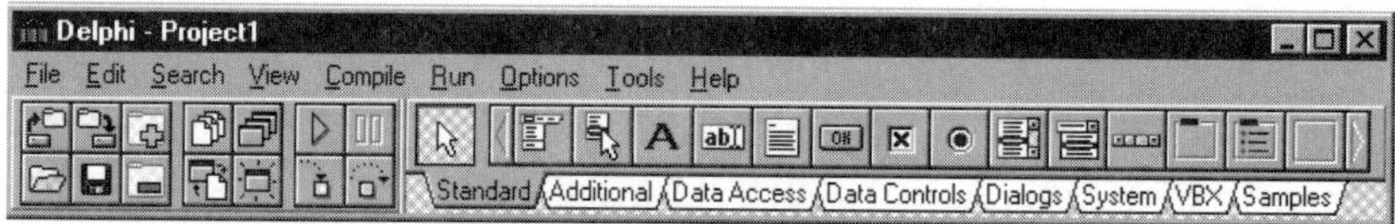

Figure 1.1 Delphi control bar (Delphi's main menu).

In addition, you will see an empty form called *Form1* and the object inspector (shown in Figure 1.2). The Delphi manual (or any Delphi programming book), talks about all the controls you can put on the form, including list boxes, push buttons, and edit windows. Of course, this seems a little pre-mature. With DOS, we tend to develop from the top down. We *will* create various screens (*forms* in Delphi parlance), but not right away. Let's first create our menu system to guide the user among the screens. The user is expected to navigate through a series of menus to get to the desired screen.

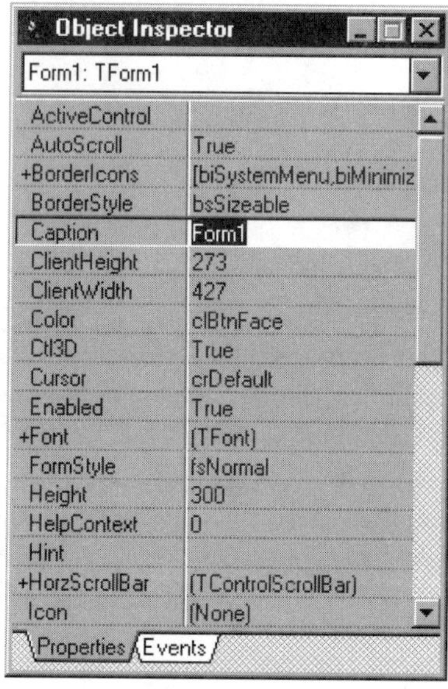

Figure 1.2 Delphi object inspector.

Thinking in DOS terms, the first form is the same as our main program. When the program starts, this is the program that gets control first. We will usually open our files and then present a menu structure for the user.

Designing the Menu System in Delphi

The first thing we need to get over is the concept of a *form*. In DOS terms, the closest thing to a form is the data entry screens. Because the screens are usually programmed after the menu has been constructed, it seems odd to begin working immediately in a form. The important thing to remember, however, is that all work in Delphi takes place within forms, and the form is not restricted to data entry screens. Even though the Delphi manual and the ease of control placement make the form seem like the DOS screen counterpart, it actually contains much more.

Each form in a Delphi program consists of a series of properties and methods. *Properties* are similar to variables in Xbase and are used to control a component's behavior. Unlike Xbase, properties are strongly typed. *Methods* are code snippets that are attached to the component and will only operate within its confines. Methods get the component to do something for you while properties provide control over how the component will behave. By modifying the property values, you can greatly control the appearance and operation of the program you are writing. Using the object inspector, it is simply a matter of locating the form's property in the object inspector and clicking on it. You can change the property's value to customize the form to your liking.

The first form that appears in Delphi, labeled *Form1*, is really the same thing as your main program in a DOS environment. Let's make a couple of changes to properties via the object inspector. Find the object property called **Caption** and change this to **Simple Accounting**. Then find the **Name** property and change this from **Form1** to **Main**. Now, we can think of this entity as a main program rather than calling it Form*1*.

We will talk about most of the other form properties in subsequent chapters. A good deal of Windows programming in Delphi and Visual Basic is accomplished by selecting and tweaking properties rather than the actual writing of code as you've done in DOS programs. While this may be disconcerting and may cause you to feel a loss of control, the more you work with this visual programming concept, the less you'll miss the manual coding of DOS languages.

Selecting the Menu Control

The next step is to find the menu control and place it on the Main form. The menu control is the first (leftmost) control in the component toolbar.

If the menu control is not the first item, select the **Standard** tab. This should cause the menu control to be the first control in the list. Figure 1.3 shows the Delphi menu control icon.

Figure 1.3 Delphi menu control icon.

Click on the menu component and place it in the Main form. The object inspector should now show a menu object and its properties. There are only four properties. The *Tag* property is used to extend the object (which we won't do for a while). The *Name* property is set to **MainMenu1**; I usually change this to **MainMenu** because the application is only going to have one main menu. You can make this change if you'd like, but the real fun begins when you click on the **Items** property. This invokes the menu editor, which is where the menu prompts and options are entered. Much of Windows programming in Delphi (and most Windows development tools) is done visually, and the menu editor is no exception. When you invoke the menu editor, the form changes to display how the menu will appear. An empty bar, as shown in Figure 1.4, appears across the top and allows you to start entering prompts.

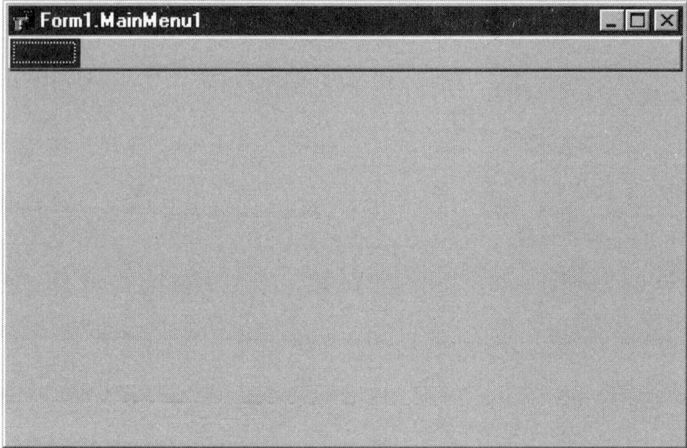

Figure 1.4 Menu designer bar.

To enter a prompt, move the mouse to the next empty square. Once you are positioned, edit the caption property in the object inspector and type the name of the prompt. You will find yourself switching back and forth between the visual menu being designed on the form and the object inspector so that you can enter the caption text. You can complete the menu in any order; you can do all the main prompts first and then the pull-downs, or vice versa. However, for now, just enter the prompts from Table 1.1; don't experiment with the other properties.

When you enter the **Financial Reporting** caption, you will need to create a submenu. To do this, click on the **Financial Reporting** prompt and then click the right mouse button. This will cause the menu shown in Figure 1.5 to appear. Select **Create Submenu** from this list, and enter the report names in a submenu next to the **Financial Reporting** prompt.

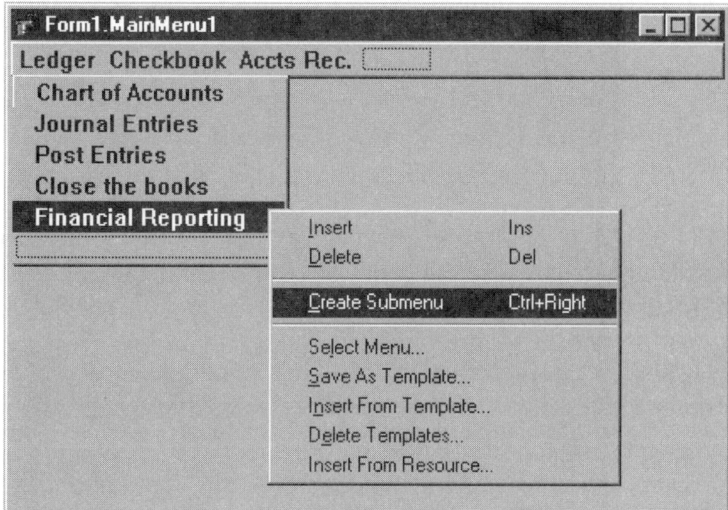

Figure 1.5 Pop-up menu.

When you are finished, the menu should look like Figure 1.6. Take your time to play with the menu editor and visually design some menus. When you've created a menu, press **F9** to compile the program. By using the menu editor and setting properties, particularly the caption, you can easily put together the menu in Delphi.

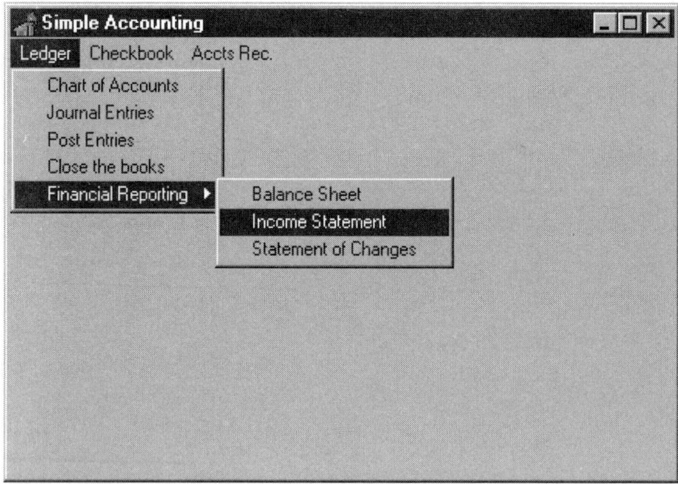

Figure 1.6 First pass at our menu.

When in Rome

Windows users expect a bit more than a simple menu system (actually, they expect a lot more, but more on that later). Let's improve our menu by adding a few features that are fairly common in Windows programs. You will need to enter the menu editor again by clicking on the **menu control** contained on the form. This will allow you to access the menu through the object inspector. As you will see, adding features and changing the menu is fairly easy using the menu editor and the object inspector. We can make a very robust menu system within Delphi without writing any code.

The following properties can all be changed to alter the appearance of your menu.

- **Caption property.** By imbedding an & character in the string, we can cause the menu to display an accelerator key. The *accelerator key* will be the character immediately following the & character and will allow the user to press **Alt** and that plus the key to jump to that menu item. Try changing your captions from **Ledger** to **&Ledger**, **Checkbook** to **&Checkbook**, and so on. Most Windows programs use accelerator keys on their menus.
- **Checked property.** This property can either be **TRUE** or **FALSE.** If **TRUE**, a check mark will appear to the right of the menu prompt. Try checking a couple of the menu prompts. A check mark is generally used to indicate that an option on a menu has been selected.

- **Enabled property**. This property is used to determine whether the user can select the menu choice. You can make a version of our accounting program that has a security system built in. You could disable the **Close the books** option for all users but the Controller or disable **Print Invoices** if there are no invoices scheduled for printing.
- **Hint property**. This property contains a text string that will appear in a bubble whenever the mouse is moved over the menu selection. This allows the user to see what trouble they might get into if they select, say the **Erase and Format Disk** option from the menu. If you enter some hint text, you must set the **ShowHint** property to **TRUE**.
- **ShortCut**. This property specifies a key stroke combination that can be used to invoke the menu option. If you click on this property, a list of available keys will appear. Select the key and the menu will be shown with the name of the key next to it. For example, try setting **Ctrl-B** as the shortcut key for the Balance Sheet and **Ctrl-I** as the shortcut to the Income Statement.

To improve our menu, we should add the standard Help menu that Windows users have come to know and love. Fortunately, this is simply a matter of placing the cursor after the last menu prompt and clicking on the right mouse. When you do this, the pop-up menu in Figure 1.7 will appear.

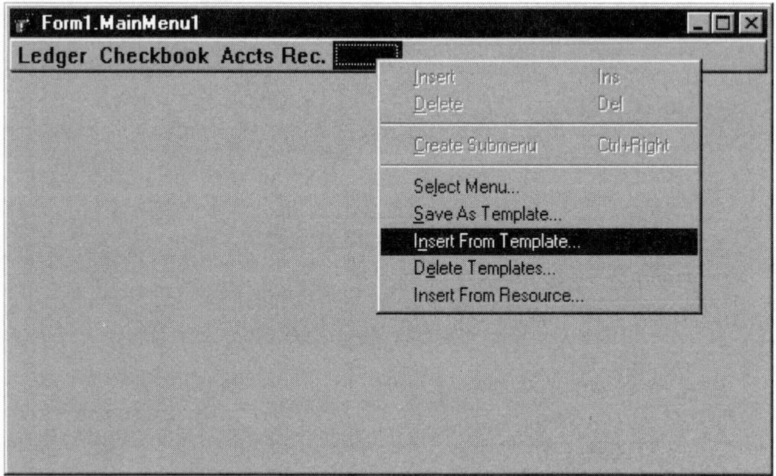

Figure 1.7 Delphi menu options.

If you select the **Insert From Template** option, a list of standard menus will be presented for you to plug into your application. Select the standard **Help** menu and insert it in your menu system. When you are finished making changes, press **F9** to compile and run the program. Your finished output should look something like Figure 1.8.

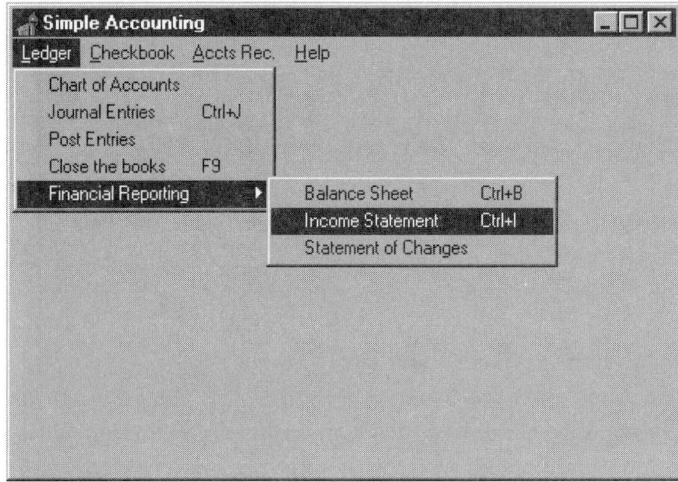

Figure 1.8 Final menu structure.

Even though we had to specify the prompt text, various accelerator keys, and hot-keys, we did not have to write any code—Delphi did it all for us.

Menuing in Visual Basic

You also can use Visual Basic to create Windows applications. Initiate Visual Basic and you will see the menu bar and buttons shown in Figure 1.9. They are similar to the Delphi IDE we discussed earlier.

Figure 1.9 Visual Basic menu/toolbar.

You will also see a form and property list, which operates in a similar way to Delphi's object inspector. Visual Basic's property list, shown in Figure 1.10, is what we use to control the appearance and operation of the program.

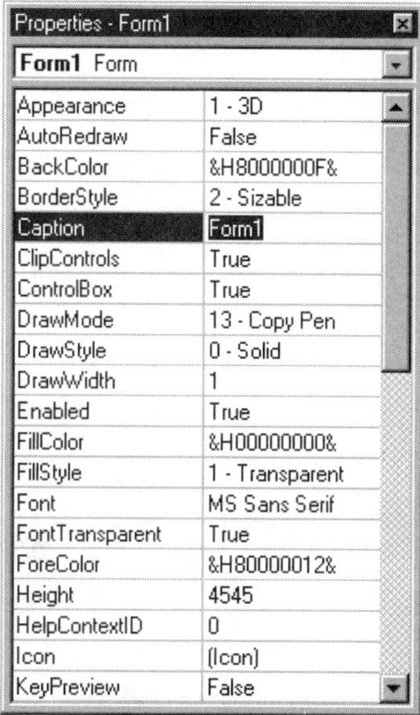

Figure 1.10 Visual Basic's property editor window.

Double-click on the **Caption** property and set the Caption value to **Simple Accounting**. In addition, change the Name property to **Main** rather than **Form*1***. After making these changes, the modified form should look like Figure 1.11.

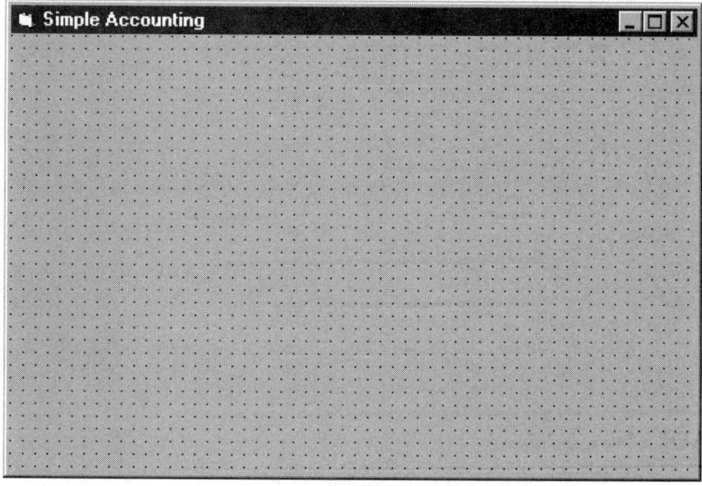

Figure 1.11 Visual Basic form.

To place our menu on the form in Visual Basic, click on the form and press **Ctrl-E** (or select **Menu designer** from the Tools drop-down menu). Note: **Ctrl-M** accesses the menu designer in Visual Basic 3.0. Figure 1.12 shows the Visual Basic menu designer.

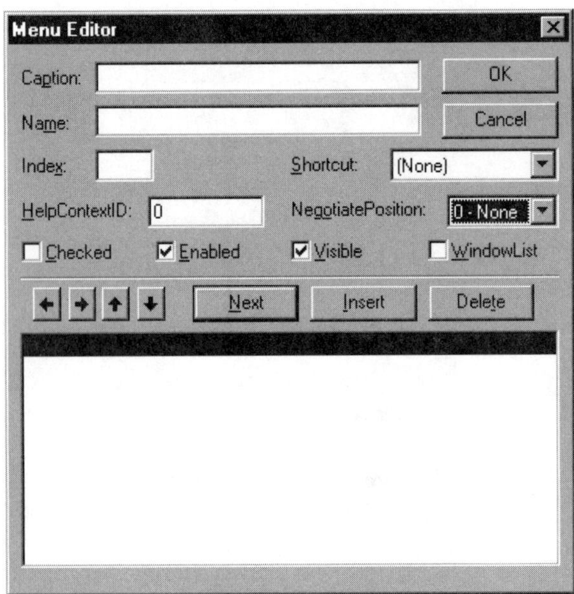

Figure 1.12 Menu Designer.

To add an entry in the menu designer, first click on the **Caption** label and enter the menu item text. You must also enter a value in the **Name** property; enter the program that will be called when the menu option is selected (for example, **UpdChart** or **Journal** at the bottom of Listing 1.1).

As you enter the captions and names from Table 1.1, the menu's contents will appear in the panel at the bottom of the designer window. You can click the **Next** button to move to the next menu option. When you are finished entering the menu captions and name, the designer should look like Figure 1.13.

Figure 1.13 Completed menu structure.

We can now adjust the menu list to reflect our structure. To do this, click the **Next** button. This will move the highlight bar to the **Chart of Accounts** entry. Now click on the **right arrow** button and indent *Chart of Accounts* one level. Click **Next** and repeat the process for *Journal Entries*, and so on. When you move to the three reports, **Balance Sheet, Income Statement**, and **Statement of Changes,** be sure to indent these two levels by clicking the **right arrow** button twice. Figure 1.14 shows the adjusted menu designer screen.

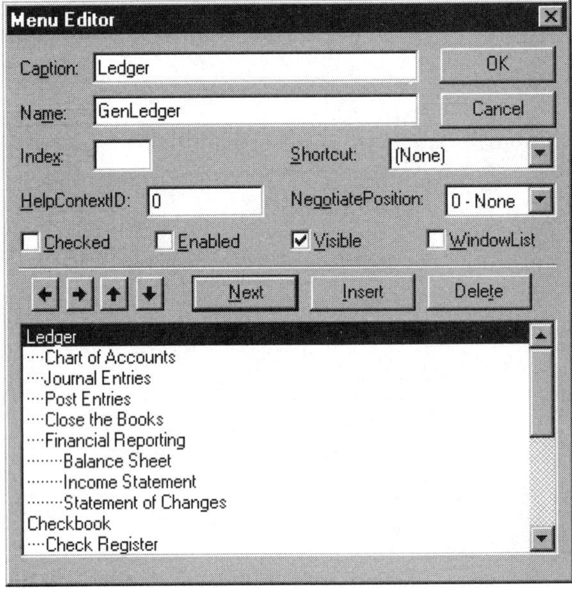

Figure 1.14 Menu designer with indented menu items.

Now, press F5 to run the program. The result should look like Figure 1.15

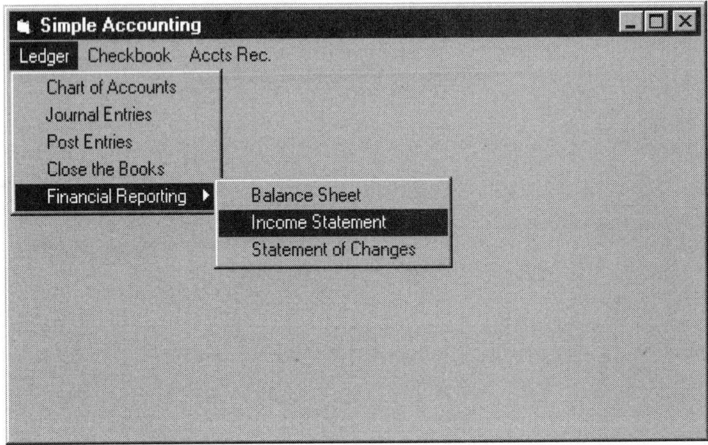

Figure 1.15 Visual Basic version of Simple Accounting.

Of course, while this menu is functional, we should spend a few moments to make it more Windows-like. This process consists of adding accelerator keys and shortcut keys to the menu. An *accelerator key* is a letter that appears underlined on the menu and allows the user to access the menu by pressing the Alt key and that letter. Accelerator keys are standard in most Windows applications. *Shortcut keys* are key strokes that allow the user to go directly to a particular menu option without traversing the menu structure.

To assign an accelerator key, edit the caption text and precede the letter you want to use with an ampersand character (&). For example, change the **Ledger** caption to **&Ledger**; the **L** will appear underlined. If the user presses **Alt-L**, he or she will jump directly to that menu option.

You can also add shortcut keys to any menu option by accessing the Shortcut list box on the menu designer. When you are in this box, click on the **arrow** to its right and select the key stroke you want to enable as a shortcut. Try making the **Ctrl-J** key serve as a shortcut to **Journal Entries** and **Ctrl-B** as a shortcut to the **Balance Sheet** report.

In addition to assigning accelerator keys and hot keys, most Windows application have a standard Help menu. Although we are not going to make use of it in this chapter, lets add one for consistency. Go back to the menu designed and insert the following menu structure after the last menu choice.

Menu Caption	Hot Key
&Help	None
...&Contents	
...&Search for Help On	F1
...&Using Help	
———————————-	
...&About Simple Accounting	Ctrl-A

The line of dashes is a separator and can be added by placing a single hyphen in the menu item's caption text. Separators don't do anything other than break your menu into more logical groups.

When you are finishing adding keys and help, press F5 to view the results. Figure 1.16 shows the final version of our menu structure.

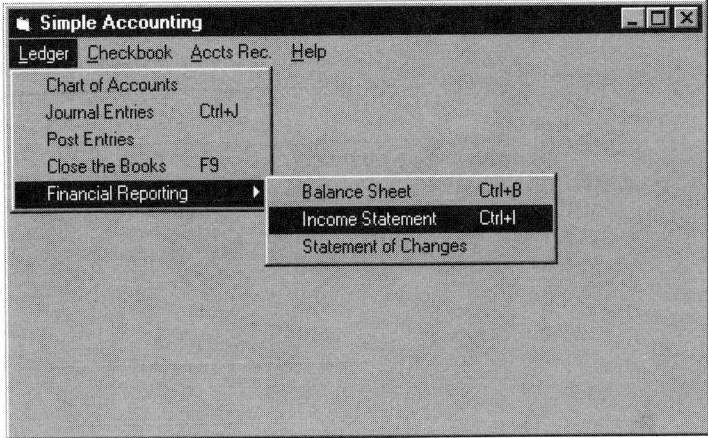

Figure 1.16 Final version of Simple Accounting menu system.

Making Things More Windows-Like

There are a few rules of thumb you should consider when designing menus, accelerator keys, and shortcut keys. While these are not set in stone, most Windows applications use them. Unless you have some burning desire to set up your own standards, take advantage of what users are used to. This will make it easier for newcomers to work with your application.

Top Menu Bar

Try to keep the top bar options short, ideally a single word. Spaces might make it hard to distinguish between options and two-word prompts. Make sure each menu option has an accelerator key associated with it, ideally the first letter in the menu prompt. Be sure to have a Help menu option and that it is the rightmost choice.

Standard Menu Items

Almost every Windows application has certain standard menu items. The Help menu is a good example; it should be included in your menu structure. The last Help menu item should always be ***About <program>***, which allows the user to find out information about the program. You should include your About Box program in this spot as well.

In addition, the last item on the first drop-down menu is usually the **E&xit** option, with the hot-key of **Alt-F4**. Place it there in all your applications. This is where users expect to find it if when they want to leave your program.

Standard Hot-Keys

The hot-keys listed in Table 1.2 are frequently used in applications. Although there is no official standard, you should try to stick with these.

Table 1.2 Common Hot-Keys

Hot-key	Purpose
Alt-F4	Exit the application
F1	Get help about the application
F10	Activate the program's menu bar
Ctrl-O	Open a document/, file/, account, etc.
Ctrl-P	Print something
Ctrl-S	Save the current item
Ctrl-Z	Undo the last operation
Ctrl-X	Cut
Ctrl-C	Copy
Ctrl-V	Paste

Try to provide short-cut keys for the most frequently used menu options. Stay away from the use of **Alt-** key combinations, because these are used for menu accelerator keys.

Many of these keys and standards can be found in *The Windows Interface: An application Design Guide* published by Microsoft Press.

Take the time to look at the menus in various Windows programs, including Visual Basic and Delphi. Get a sense of the general layout, appearance, and key usage. Try to emulate the commonality you find. It will make your users more comfortable with your system.

Summary

Creating menus in Windows is fairly easy. Take time to explore the menu editors and tools of whichever Windows tool you are using. You will soon be able to put together complete menuing systems. In the next chapter, we will begin to design screens and explore how to invoke these screens when a menu option is selected.

CHAPTER 2:

EXPLORING THE FORM

In the first chapter, we discussed how to take a simple DOS menu structure and implement it in either Delphi or Visual Basic. We also touched upon the concept of the form and made some minor changes to it. In this chapter, we will elaborate on the myriad of form options and how to use them to control your application.

Programming in Windows

When writing programs to be run in DOS, we count on pretty much having the machine's undivided attention. Our program controls the screen, access to the disk, and all inputs. Part of the challenge of programming for DOS is the careful screen design work and input processing that must be completed. For the most part, a DOS program provides a series of menus that leads to a dedicated screen that is focused on one task. To use our program, the user agrees to find the appropriate screen, restrict his or her work to completing that screen, and then navigate back through the menu to the next screen.

In such an environment, our code has complete control over (and responsibility for) the screen layout and appearance, keystroke processing, and so on. You can choose a green text against a red background if you are in a particularly sadistic mood, or you can choose the more readable white text on blue background. You can have the **Tab** key move between inputs and the **Enter** key process the inputs if you choose; the handling is all processed by your program.

Many times, users are allowed to set their own desired color schemes and even remap our keystroke handling. Of course, this complete control and responsibility of the screen and inputs can be either tedious or cause you to look at screen painting tools. Very few FoxPro programmer's write their @ SAY and @ GET commands manually; instead most rely on FoxPro's Form Designer and Form Wizards.

With Windows, you surrender that control—and the corresponding headaches—to Windows. All work within the application takes place within a window or a form as the window is often called. Windows has complete control over those forms, from controlling their color and appearance to the way keystrokes and the mouse interact with them. However, the form's appearance and interaction within your program can still be controlled. This requires setting various properties to achieve the desired behavior.

Using the Form

Figure 2.1 shows a standard Window generated by Delphi or another Windows programming language. The window has several components that you can easily control by understanding how the properties interact with Windows.

Figure 2.1 Standard window.

The standard window consists of a border drawn around the window, a title bar at the top with caption text inside it, and several buttons. Each component can be controlled to allow defining a window appropriate for most every situation.

The image in the upper left-most corner, preceding the form's title, is called the *control box* or *system menu*.. It permits the user to perform actions on the form by selecting them from a menu.

In Windows 3.x, the *system menu* consists of consists of a square box with a horizontal bar in it. Figure 2.2 shows the *system menu* box, which performs the same function regardless of the Windows version. Representing the system menu box with a small image is more in keeping with the CUA standard from IBM.

Figure 2.2 Windows 3.x system menu box.

The upper right-most corner contains a *minimize* box—which reduces the form to a small icon that represents it—and a *maximize* box—which increases the form size to fill the entire screen. For applications running under Windows 95, there will also be a *close* button, the box that has an X mark in it. Under Windows 3.x, windows were closed through the *system menu* or by the **Alt-F4** keystroke. The **close** button in Windows 95 provides a third way to close any window.

You can find these standard features in almost any Windows application. If you are not familiar with them, take the time to explore the various boxes in Visual Basic or Delphi (which are Windows applications). A basic understanding of the options allows you to decide which options to let your users have access. As a general rule of thumb, each window should have all of these controls enabled; i.e., don't restrict what the user can do with the window.

DOS Forms

Imagine in our DOS application that we've written a standard function that draws our screens for us. The function DrawBox() shown in Listing 2.1 shows an Xbase program to handle our screen drawing.

Listing 2.1 DrawBox().

```
*   Function:  Drawbox()
*   Arguments:  caption     (C) - label for the box
*              borderstyle (N) - 0=None,1=Single,2=Double
*              color       (C) - Color string
*              full_screen (L) - full screen mode ?
*              t           (N) - top screen row
*              l           (N) - screen left most corner
*              h           (N) - height of screen
*              w           (N) - width of screen
*
function DrawBox
```

```
parameters caption, borderstyle, color, full_screen,t,l,h,w

if full_screen
    t  = 0          && Default values for full screen mode
    l  = 0
    h  = maxrow()
    w  = maxcol()
endif
set color to &color
@ t,l clear to t+h,l+w
do case
case borderstyle = 0        && No border at all
case borderstyle = 1        && Single line border
   @ t,l to t+h,l+w
   @ t,l+(w/2)-(len(caption)/2) say " "+caption+" "
case borderstyle = 2        && Double line border
   @ t,l to t+h,l+w double
   @ t,l+(w/2)-(len(caption)/2) say " "+caption+" "
otherwise                   && Default to single line
   @ t,l to t+h,l+w
   @ t,l+(w/2)-(len(caption)/2) say " "+caption+" "
endcase
return .T.
```

We could easily plug this function into our menu code from Listing 1.1 in the first chapter. We would then add the following lines of code to setup our application prior to calling the menu system.

```
***********************************************
* Clear the screen and display the initial box *
***********************************************
clear screen
DrawBox( "Simple Accounting", 2 , "W/B" ,.T. )
```

Windows programming, in essence, provides such a function, which will automatically get called whenever the window needs to be displayed. However, instead of sending arguments to the function, various form properties will be set to determine how the window appears and operates.

Although this book focuses on Visual Basic and Delphi, the concept of setting properties to control a window's appearance and behavior exists even when you use C or C++ to code your Windows application.

Controlling Your Main Form in Windows

With either Visual Basic or Delphi, you need to call up the property inspector and tweak some properties to get the desired window. This is like changing the parameters you pass to the DrawBox() function in Listing 2.1.

Figure 2.3 shows the object inspector from Delphi and Figure 2.4 shows the property editor from Visual Basic.

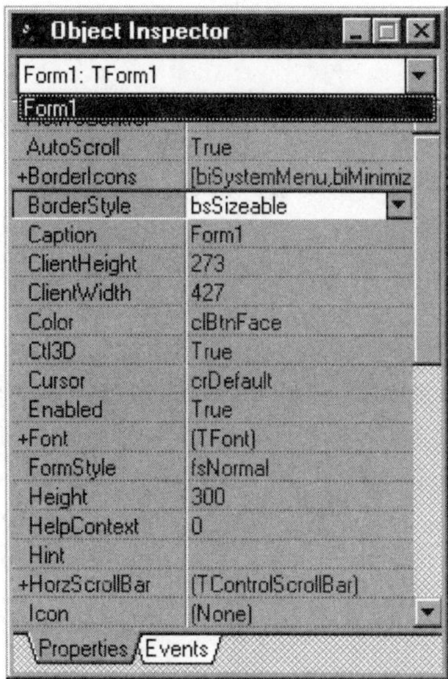

Figure 2.3 Delphi Object Inspector.

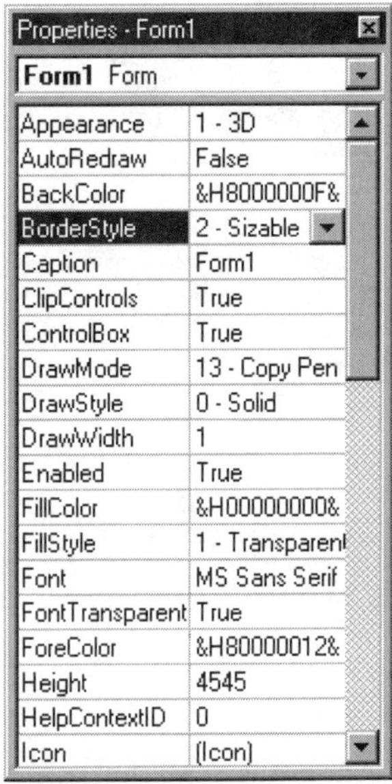

Figure 2.4 Visual Basic Property editor.

Common Properties

A few of the form properties are the most common ones you will need to change. At this point, explore these properties and see the impact changing them makes on your screen design. In Chapter 4 we will spend much more time examining form properties and controls.

BorderStyle

The *borderstyle* property determines the border that is seen by the user. However, the type of border also determines what features are allowed within the window. For example, a **Sizable** border, the default in both Visual Basic and Delphi, will cause the window to include a control box, a title bar, a minimize button, and a maximize button. The user can move or resize the form, as well as minimize it (reduce it to an icon symbol) or maximize it—make the form take up the entire screen.

Visual Basic has the following six options for border styles:

(0) **None** No border is drawn, no control box, title, or minimize/maximize buttons are included. The end-user will not be able to see the form, although components placed on the form will be visible.

(1) **FixedSingle** A single line border is drawn around the frame, along with a title bar, a control box, and minimize and maximize buttons. The user can move, minimize, and maximize, but not resize it.

(2) **Sizable** (Visual Basic's default borderstyle) Basically allows everything. It has a title bar, control box, and minimize and maximize buttons. The user may adjust the size or move the form to their heart's content. The border consists of a double line. This is a standard in Windows that indicates the box can be moved and sized.

(3) **FixedDouble** This option includes a control box and a title bar, but is not resizable. It does not include a minimize or maximize button. In general, this type of border is used to show dialog boxes. Dialog boxes are generally modal (i.e., the user must process the box to continue).

(4) **Fixed ToolWindow** Similar to FixedSingle, except a smaller font is used in the title bar and the window does not appear in the taskbar. This option only works with Windows 95 and Windows NT 3.51 or later releases.

(5) **Sizable ToolWindow** Similar to Fixed ToolWindow except that the window can be resized. This option only works with Windows 95 and Windows NT 3.51 or later releases.

Delphi also supports these six border styles, with slightly different names, listed here:

(0) **bsNone** No border is drawn, no control box, title, or minimize and maximize buttons. The end user will not be able to see the form, although components placed on the form will be visible.

(1) **bsSingle** A single line border is drawn around the frame, along with a title bar, a control box, and a minimize/maximize pair. The user can move the form around, minimize, and maximize it, but not resize it.

(2) **bsSizeable** (Delphi's default borderstyle) Basically allows everything. It has a title bar, control box, and minimize and maximize buttons. The user may size or move the form to their heart's content. The border consists of a double line. This is a standard in Windows that indicates the box can be moved and sized.

(3) **bsDialog** This option includes a control box and a title bar, but is not resizable. It does not include a minimize or maximize buttons. In general, this type of border is used to show dialog boxes.

(4) **bsToolWindow** Similar to bsSingle, except a smaller font is used in the title bar and the window does not appear in the taskbar. This option only works with Windows 95 and Windows NT 3.51 or later releases.

(5) **bsSizeToolWin** Similar to bsToolWindow except that the window can be resized. This option only works with Windows 95 and Windows NT 3.51 or later releases.

The main form and most forms within applications should be very permissive. Windows users are accustomed to sizing and moving forms all over the place. Your program should accommodate them.

However, if you hit a situation that warrants immediate attention, you should use a borderstyle that cannot be minimized or sized to oblivion. These kinds of situations—such as the printer running out of paper, or the user about to overwrite a file—should use the ***Fixed Double*** or ***bsDialog*** style.

Caption

The **caption** property is used to assign a title to the window. If the window's border style supports a title bar, it is the caption text that will be displayed in it. This is the same property name in both Delphi and Visual Basic.

Try to assign a short caption name to every window in your application. In addition, if the window is processing a single item, that item's name should be part of the caption text. The Ami Pro word processing package provides an example by using the caption 'Ami Pro - [<document>]' in its main window. This allows the user to clearly see the open windows if he or she calls up the task list. Figure 2.5 shows an example of the task list box of Windows 3.x.

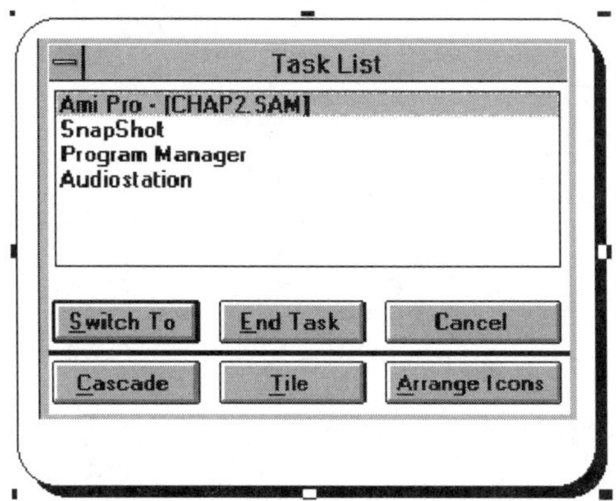

Figure 2.5 Sample task list.

For Windows 95, the task list window has been replaced with the task bar that appears on the bottom of the screen. Figure 2.6 shows the Windows 95 taskbar.

Figure 2.6 Windows 95 task bar.

In Visual Basic 4.x, a new property called **ShowInTaskBar** has been introduced. It controls whether or not this window name should be shown in the task bar. The default is FALSE, so only windows you explicitly set to TRUE will appear in the Windows 95 task bar.

ControlBox

The **control box** symbol appears in the upper left-hand corner of the window. It is used to allow the user to move or size the window, as well as minimize it, or maximize it. Figure 2.5 shows a sample control box which appears if the user clicks on the control box symbol or presses the Alt-space bar combination.

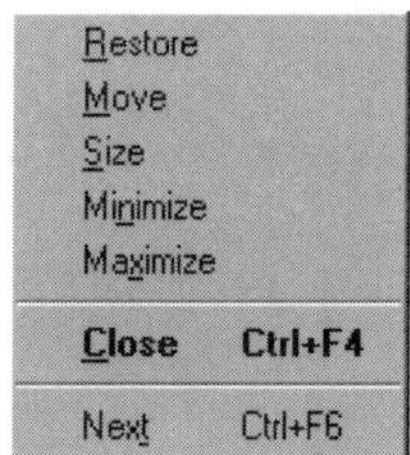

Figure 2.7 Control box.

Any menu option in the control box which is not allowed will be grayed out and not selectable. The restore option is used to return the window to normal size after it has been minimized or maximized.

Visual Basic has a property called **ControlBox** which can be set to TRUE to enable the ***control box*** (or ***system menu***) and FALSE to disable it. In Delphi, the **Control Box** option (called ***biSystemMenu***) as well as the minimize and maximize (called **biMinimize** and **biMaximize,** respectively) buttons are hidden under the **BorderIcon** property. You need to click on the **plus** sign to the left of **BorderIcons** to expose the options underneath. Figure 2.8 shows the Delphi property inspector with the **BorderIcons** property expanded.

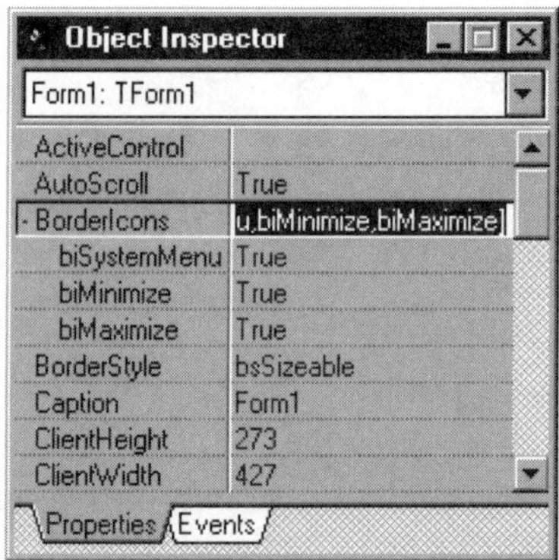

Figure 2.8 Delphi property inspector, with expanded BorderIcons.

Ctl3d (Delphi) /Appearance (Visual Basic)

This property determines whether the window should have a three-dimensional appearance or not. In Delphi, **Ctl3D** contains a TRUE value if you want to have a three-dimensional, sculpted appearance to the form. If set to FALSE, the control have a two-dimensional appearance. In Visual Basic, **Appearance** contains 1-3D to enable three dimensional effects, or 0-Flat to disable them.

I recommend leaving the 3-D property enabled, but that is strictly a matter of aesthetics.

Icon

The **icon** property indicates which graphic bitmap file should be used to represent the window when it is minimized. While there is no counterpart to the icon in DOS programming, icons and graphic representations of objects are standard for Windows programming. Figures 2.9 and 2.10 show some familiar Windows icons for Windows 3.x. Windows 95 places minimized windows in the task bar next to a very small icon symbol. If you anticipate that the user is likely to minimize windows within your application, then choose a bitmap graphic to help them remember what type of window was minimized, i.e., was the window a graph, a letter, a file, a document, and so on.

Figure 2.9 Visual Basic's Icon.

Figure 2.10 Delphi's Icon.

Minimize Button

The **minimize** button appears in the upper right-hand corner of the window. It allows the user to reduce the window to an icon. The user does not have to deal with this window right now, but keep it in sight until he or she wants to work with it.

For the most part, your main form should always have a **minimize** button. However, any critical dialog box, such as a warning that you are about to erase a file or that Windows is about to crash, should not be able to be tucked away and ignored.

In Visual Basic, the **MinButton** property can be used to control whether or not a box has a minimize button. TRUE adds a minimize button and FALSE excludes it. In Delphi, the **biMinimize** option is hidden under the **BorderIcon's** property. See Figure 2.8.

Maximize Button

The **maximize** button also appears in the upper right-hand corner of the window. It is used to allow the user to increase the window to the full screen size. This allows the user to blot out from view everything else and concentrate on this window.

In Visual Basic, the **MaxButton** property can be used to control whether or not a box has a maximize button. TRUE adds a maximize button and FALSE excludes it. In Delphi, the **biMaximize** option is hidden under the **BorderIcon's** property. See Figure 2.8.

We can mimic the maximize behavior in a DOS application as shown in Listing 2.2:

Listing 2.2 Maximize option in a DOS program.

```
* Example Clipper code to maximize a TBROWSE window
*
oBrow := TbrowseDB( 8,20,18,60 )  && 10 rows by 40 cols
while .T.              && Annoy the coding purists
     x = inkey(500)
     do case
     case x = MAXIMIZE_BUTTON

        oBrow:nLeft    = 0
        oBrow:nTop     = 0
        oBrow:nRight   = maxcol()
        oBrow:nBottom  = Maxrow()
        oBrow:reconfigure()
        oBrow:refreshAll()
        loop
     case....
enddo
```

Considering the complexity of trying to maximize a screen of SAYs and GETs, creates an appreciation of the amount work Windows does behind the scenes.

Colors

In most DOS programming, it is the programmers' responsibility to select the color scheme. Many have turned this duty over to the end user by given them the ability to control colors. Of course, as you can see from Figure 2.11. Window's users already have control over their color settings.

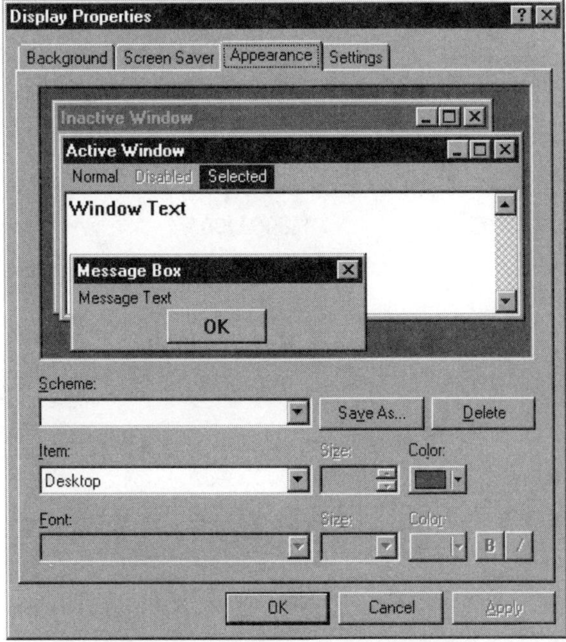

Figure 2.11 Windows color setting.

While it is possible for you to take total control of the forms' color scheme, it is best to leave color selection to the user and Windows. In this section, we will explore how to control the form colors.

Visual Basic allows you to control the foreground and background colors using the **ForeColor** and **BackColor** properties respectively. When dealing with any color properties, a numeric value to indicate the color to use. Two ways exist to determine this color.

Use Colors from the Control Panel

Figure 2.11 illustrates a listbox entitled ***Item*** (which currently contains Desktop). This listbox allows the user to select which element of the screen color they want to change.

The listbox provides control over everything from the background and foreground colors to the color of shadows to draw on command buttons. You can access these elements by assigning manifest constants to the appropriate color property. Table 2.1 lists the manifest constants available in Visual Basic.

Table 2.1 Color manifest constants

SCROLL_BARS	&H80000000 '	Scroll-bars gray area
DESKTOP	&H80000001 '	Desktop
ACTIVE_TITLE_BAR	&H80000002 '	Active window caption
INACTIVE_TITLE_BAR	&H80000003 '	Inactive window caption
MENU_BAR	&H80000004 '	Menu background
WINDOW_BACKGROUND	&H80000005 '	Window background
WINDOW_FRAME	&H80000006 '	Window frame
MENU_TEXT	&H80000007 '	Text in menu
WINDOW_TEXT	&H80000008 '	Text in windows
TITLE_BAR_TEXT	&H80000009 '	Text in caption, size box, scroll-bar arrow box
ACTIVE_BORDER	&H8000000A '	Active window border
INACTIVE_BORDER	&H8000000B '	Inactive window border
APPLICATION_WORKSPACE	&H8000000C '	Background color of MDI
HIGHLIGHT	&H8000000D '	Selected item in a control
HIGHLIGHT_TEXT	&H8000000E '	Text selected in a control
BUTTON_FACE	&H8000000F '	Face shading on buttons
BUTTON_SHADOW	&H80000010 '	Edge shading on buttons
GRAY_TEXT	&H80000011 '	Grayed (disabled) text
BUTTON_TEXT	&H80000012 '	Text on push buttons

The cryptic looking numbers starting with &H8 are hexadecimal values that represent which screen element from the control panel to use. The defaults are **WINDOW_BACKGROUND**

(&H80000005) for the BackColor property and **WINDOW_TEXT** (&H0000008) for the ForeColor property.

Creating Your Own Colors

If you are adventurous, or feeling somewhat artistic, you can assign your own color set to the form's background and foreground. Colors in Windows parlance are derived by mixing the three primary colors (Red, Green, and Blue) in varying amount to produce an almost infinite number of colors.

Visual Basic provides a function called RGB() which allows you to specify the mix. The function returns a numeric value that Visual Basic interprets as a color. The function syntax is:

```
nColor   = RGB(   red,  green,  blue  )
```

where : ***red*** is an integer between 0 and 255 that indicates the mix of the red color.

green is an integer between 0 and 255 that indicates the mix of the green color.

blue is an integer between 0 and 255 that indicates the mix of the blue color.

The result of this function is a hexidecimal number that produces some shade of color. Table 2.2 lists some common colors:

Table 2.2 Common colors

Color	Hex number	Red	Green	Blue
Black	&H00	0	0	0
Blue	&H00	0	0	255
Green	&H00	0	255	0
Cyan	&H00	0	255	255
Red	&H00	255	0	255
Magenta	&H00	255	0	0
Yellow	&HFFFF	255	255	0
White	&HFFFFFF	255	255	255

Windows will match your combination of red, green, and blue to the closest color that the adapter can display. If you feel that you need absolute color control in your form, you can have it. Remember that Windows users are used to having control over such aspects and your application might not be well received if you take away that control. On the other hand, if the color of the screen indicates the severity of problems at a nuclear power plant, please, by all means, leave it in.

Delphi Color Control

Delphi's background color is controlled via a form property called *color*. The foreground color is tucked away under the **font** property, i.e., font color. Both of these properties have an enumerated list available for selecting colors. The first 18 choices on the list are constant color specifications which result in color selections that cannot be changed by the end user (unless you build that option into your program). The second group are the colors from the control panel that the user can change through Windows. Table 2.3 lists Delphi's color options.

Table 2.3 Delphi Color Options

clAqua	clGray	clNavy	clTeal
clBlack	clGreen	clOlive	clWhite
clBlue	clLime	clPurple	clYellow
clDkGray	clLtGray	clRed	
clFuchsia	clMaroon	clSilver	
clActiveBorder	clActiveCaption	clAppWorkSpace	
clBackground	clBtnFace	clBtnHighlight	
clBtnShadow	clBtnText	clCaptionText	
clGrayText	clHighlight	clInactiveBorder	
clInactiveCaption	clInactiveCaptionText	clMenu	
clMenuText	clScrollBar	clWindow	
clWindowFrame	clWindowText		

If you want to hard-code colors into your application, be sure to have a good reason for doing so. Windows users are used to a large degree of flexibility in their applications and that shouldn't be taken away from them.

WindowState

The **windowstate** property determines how the window should appear when the program first starts. There are three possible options:

Normal—The window appears whatever size you designed. This is controlled by the top, left, height, and width properties.

Minimized—The window appears as an icon symbol to start.

Maximized—The window occupies the entire screen when the program starts. Although this is the mode you've probably gotten accustomed to in DOS, try to keep in mind that most Windows uses expect to be able to see their other programs behind yours.

In Delphi, the property values are **wsNormal, wsMinimized**, and **wsMaximized**. In Visual Basic, they are **0-normal, 1-minimized**, and **2-maximized.**

For the most part, leave this set at **normal**. However if you want your application to blot out any other open windows, then set this property to maximized.

Summary

Hopefully this chapter has given you an idea of the breadth of what you need to take care of when programming in Windows. While the visual programming tools make everything easily accessible, there is a large number of properties for you to control. You can control the appearance and operation of any screen or form within a Windows program fairly easily by setting values in various form properties. Explore the Windows tool to see the variety of forms you can create and the impact of changing all those properties. Once you feel comfortable tweaking properties and forms, go on to Chapter 3, which tells how to design a user interface for the Windows environment and explains why we need all those properties.

CHAPTER 3:
Common User Access

When you first open Delphi or Visual Basic, you will notice a multitude of different methods for interacting with the user. Icons, mouse cursors, list boxes, radio buttons, combo boxes, and pop-up menus are a few examples. The sheer number of options can be intimidating to a DOS developer, raising questions such as: When do I use which component? What goes on the menu and what doesn't? How do I decide which icon to use to represent a form?

Fortunately, Windows programming comes with some guidelines. These guidelines are based upon Common User Access (CUA).

What Exactly is CUA?

In early 1987, IBM introduced a strategy for creating multiplatform software systems. This strategy was called Systems Application Architecture (SAA). The intent of the strategy was to make software developers and users more productive by providing consistent interfaces across hardware and software platforms. CUA is one component of SAA, the component that deals with the end user's view and interaction with the software.

CUA is a set of guidelines suggesting how to present a program's functionality to the end user. Programs based on CUA guidelines run consistently, which makes interaction easier for the end user. A user working with the Ami-Pro word processor could easily switch to Microsoft Word, since both interfaces are CUA-based. This is similar to how cars are designed. The placement of the steering wheel, gas pedal, brake, and the standard features are consistent, allowing most people to drive any type of automobile without requiring new training .

Does CUA work? Microsoft Windows is based upon CUA and could be considered a successful example of CUA at work. By following the guidelines of CUA, applications can be produced that are easier to use and require less training. This chapter discusses the CUA guidelines and how they fit in using Delphi or Visual Basic. By following the CUA guidelines, you can produce applications that feel like Windows programs, not just programs ported from DOS.

Changing the System View

CUA views the programming differently than it would be in DOS. In a DOS program, the program is organized by functionality and then mapped onto a menu structure. Under CUA guidelines, the view of the program changes to more accurately reflect how the user interacts with the program.

Objects

When users work without a computer, they generally work with objects of some kind. An architect uses a T-square, blueprints, and pencils. An accountant uses ledgers and journals. CUA is an object-based software view; the user expects to see computer representations of objects he or she might use, and to be able to interact with these objects. For a good example, look at the popular paint accessory program that comes with Windows (see Figure 3.1). In this type of program the screen contains an object that corresponds to a canvas and a number of objects for drawing on the canvas, i.e., erasers, pencils, and paintbrushes.

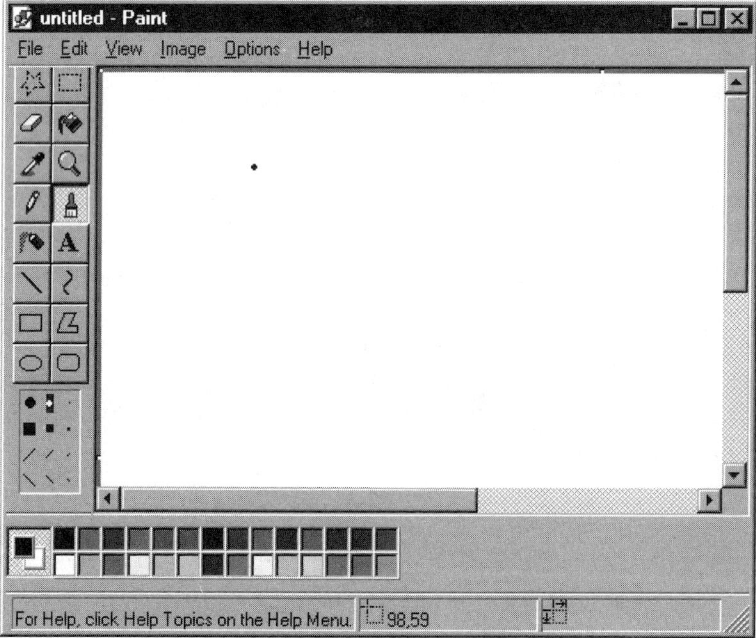

Figure 3.1 Paint Accessory program.

Object Types

There are three types of objects that can be represented in CUA. The first is a *data object*. Its purpose is to convey information to the user. The information can be in graphic form, such as a bitmap image, or textual. Checks, receipts, and photographs are examples of data objects.

The second type of object is a *container object*. This object consists of a group of data objects, such as a photo album, a portfolio, or a general ledger (containing a number of accounts). A container object allows transactions to be performed against all objects in the container, while also allowing the user to extract individual objects from the container and work with them.

The third object is a *device object*, which represents some physical object, such as a printer or a modem. A device object might contain other objects, such as a print queue that contains a number of documents waiting to be printed, or an in-bin with unopened emails.

Creating an Object View

To design a CUA-based program, the objects that the system is going to manipulate must be analyzed. In Chapter One, we designed a menu structure describing the system's functionality. This has been expanded and repeated below.

General Ledger

```
   Edit Chart of Accounts
   Record Journal Entries
   Post Entries
   Close the Books
   Financial Reporting
        Balance Sheet
        Income Statement
     Statement of Changes in Financial Position
  Checkbook
   Check Register
   Pay Bills
   Print Checks
   Make Deposits
   Bank Reconciliation
```

```
Accounts Receivable/Invoicing
 Add/edit Customers
 Write Invoices
 Print Invoices
 Apply Payments
```

Although presented in menu fashion, this list is also a working list of the tasks the system needs to perform. The tasks need to be reviewed to extract the objects that the system will work with. A quick way to find the objects would be to list all of the nouns in the task list. For our accounting system, these objects might be:

From Ledger Menu

Chart of Accounts

Journals Entries

Books

Financial Reports

From Checkbook Menu

Checkbook

Bills

Checks

Deposits

Bank Reconciliation

From A/R Menu

Customers

Invoices

Payments

The object list must be reviewed for two purposes. First, any duplicate objects must be removed (i.e., Chart of Accounts and Books both refer to the ledger). Second, our objects need to be classified as either data objects (such as invoices or checks.) or container objects (such as the checkbook which contains both deposit and check objects).

Our final listing of objects appears in Table 3.1.

Table 3.1 Accounting Objects

OBJECT	Type	Description
Ledger	Container object	Books or Chart of Accounts
Accounts	Data object	One particular account
Journals	Container objects	Various system journals
Entries	Data object	Debits/Credits entries
Financial Reports	Container object	All financial reports
Balance Sheet	Data object	Balance Sheet report
Income Statement	Data object	Income statement
Statement of Changes	Data object	Statement of Changes in Financial Position
Checkbook	Container object	Company checkbook
Checks	Data object	Checks
Deposits	Data object	Deposit slips
Bills	Data object	Bills from vendors
Bank Reconciliation	Data object	Bank reconciliation paperwork
Customers	Data object	Clients we sell good/services to
Invoices	Data object	Invoices for services rendered/goods sold
Payments	Data object	Checks received from customers

CUA Components

This section looks at the components that are used in a CUA interface. All of these components can be easily assembled on a Delphi or Visual Basic form as we will see in the next chapter. The key to a good interface is putting together the components on the form that most closely mimic the process your program is performing.

Workplace

The *workplace* in a CUA application is a container provided by the operating environment where all objects reside. In Windows, this area is called the *desktop*, and occupies the entire screen. Applications reside on the desktop and when they are minimized, their icon also is placed on the desktop. In Windows 95, minimized icons are placed in a row at the bottom of the screen called the *task bar*. Figure 3.2 shows a sample task bar with three programs minimized.

Figure 3.2 Windows 95 task bar.

Windows

The workplace, or desktop in Windows parlance, consists of icons and windows. The windows are where the applications interact with the user. Each time an application is created in Visual Basic or Delphi, a main window is created. The program controls the interaction with this window and any secondary windows created. The operating system provides the standard behavior under which this window operates.

A *standard window* in CUA consists of a number of component features and operations. Most of these features can be controlled by setting property values within your application. This section briefly covers the standard window and its behaviors. Figure 3.3 shows a standard window created by Visual Basic in Windows 95.

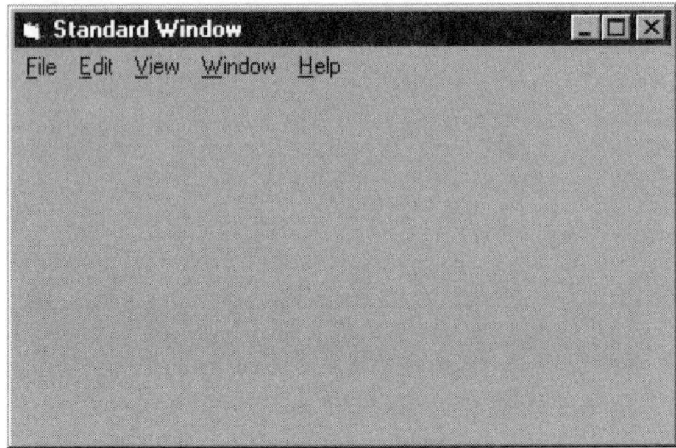

Figure 3.3 Standard CUA window.

At a minimum, each window in your application should have the following three components.

Border

The *border* is the frame drawn around the window. The border provides a visual cue as to what can be done with the window, such as minimizing it, moving it, or sizing it. In Windows, the user can move or resize the window easily using the mouse to drag the border. The various borderstyle properties in your application determine what the user can do with the window.

Title Bar

Every window should have a *title bar*, which is the small icon and caption text across the top of the window. The *caption* property in both Visual Basic and Delphi is used to specify the name of the window. The title for the main form should reflect the application name, with the first letter capitalized. If the program opens multiple documents or objects, then the title should also provide some indication of the window's current contents. For example,

Calculator		Windows **Calculator** program
NotePad	**[Phone.crd]**	**Notepad** program, with **Phone.crd** loaded

If a secondary window is opened from the main program, it should contain the application's name followed by the purpose of the window. For example,

Word	**Open**	Microsoft Word's **Open** file dialog box
Ami Pro	**Save As**	Ami Pro's **Save As** dialog box

Keep in mind that the user can resize and minimize the application's windows. Try to provide enough information in the title for the user to easily determine the correct window to restore.

System Menu

The *system* menu is a pop-up menu that allows the user to manipulate the window without relying solely on the mouse. Windows takes care of the interaction of the system menu automatically, as long as you attach one to your windows. This is the default in both Delphi and Visual Basic. The user can access the system menu by pressing **Alt-space** or by clicking the mouse on the **title bars** icon (or the **system menu** icon in Windows 3.x).

In addition to these three components, the window should also have the following standard behaviors. A good amount of this behavior is provided automatically by the Windows operating system.

Closing a Window

The window should be closed if the user clicks on the **close** button or selects **close** from the system menu. This behavior is provided automatically by Windows, but not all users know these options. A push button should be included on the window that allows the user to close it. Additionally, once the window accomplishes the task it was created to do, it should close automatically.

Sizing and Moving Windows

CUA guidelines recommend that the user be able to *size* and/or *move* the window, which is the default behavior in both Visual Basic and Delphi. In addition, if the window is minimized or maximized, the user should be able to restore it to its previous size and position. Since Windows users expect to be able to manipulate the windows, applications should allow as much window manipulation as possible. DOS programmers tend to think of screens as modal, i.e., the user must complete the window before proceeding. In CUA, this is not the case. The only time a window should be restricted is for conditions that, if ignored, would prevent the system from running, such as a printer error or a disk full situation.

Sizing Buttons

The system menu provides one method of minimizing and maximizing windows, the *sizing buttons* provide another. Visual Basic and Delphi will automatically place these buttons on the window if the border style includes them. Each button can be overridden individually, but they should rarely be excluded.

Scroll Bars

Scroll bars are components which visually indicate to the user that more information is available in a particular direction. The user can then click on the scroll bar arrows or move the scroll shaft to access the information. Scroll bars should be attached any time the window is not large enough to display all of the form's content (such as a memo field entry).

Figure 3.4 shows an example of a window with scroll bars attached to it. Fortunately, Windows will handle all interaction with the scroll bar, and both Delphi and Visual Basic allow you to easily attach scroll bars to any form.

Figure 3.4 Window with scroll bars.

Icons

Icons are small graphic images that represent some aspect of your application. Each application designed will have an icon associated with its main form. This icon will appear on the Windows desktop whenever the application is minimized. If possible, the icon should serve as a reminder to the user of what the minimized application is.

Figure 3.5 shows some minimized icons from Windows 95. Notice that each contains a small icon symbol and some text describing the minimized window.

Figure 3.5 Sample icons.

Menus

The *menu* control provides a pull-down menu structure to provide assistance to the user in navigating your application. The top line of the menu is called the *menu bar* and is positioned directly below the windows title bar. Each entry in the menu bar should lead to a pull-down menu which will appear below it. While menus are not necessary in a CUA application, they should be provided to help users work through the system.

Some standard CUA pull-down menus should be included if your application provides the associated function. These are the *File*, *Edit*, *View*, *Windows*, and *Help* menus. These menus and their contents are discussed in more detail in Chapter 5. Figure 3.6 shows a standard menu bar with the file pull-down menu exposed.

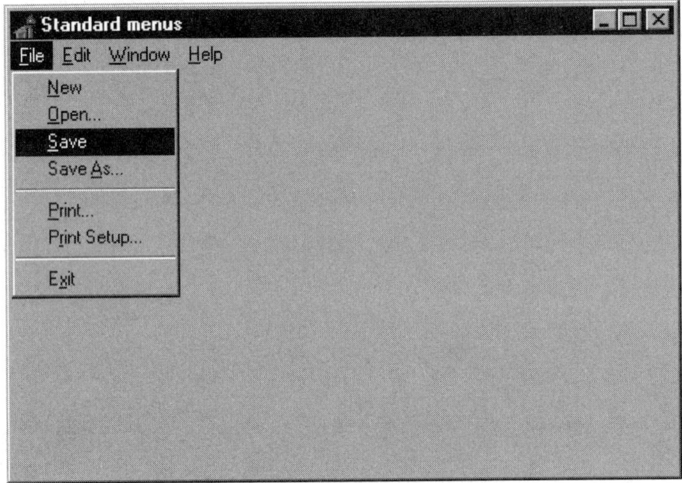

Figure 3.6 Standard menu structure.

Some Guidelines You Should Keep in Mind When Designing Menus

Try to fit application appropriate options onto the standard *File*, *Edit*, *View*, *Window*, and *Help* menus whenever possible. If the application needs other menu bar options, place those options between the **View** menu and the **Window** menu. If these options weren't used, place the specific options between the last option and the **Help** prompt.

Use the first letter or a meaningful letter as an accelerator key for each menu option. Recall from Chapter 1 that an accelerator key allows the user to press **Alt** and the letter to quickly access the menu option.

Capitalize the first letter of each option on the menu bar.

If a user should not have access to any of the options on the pull-down menu, then do not include that menu option on the menu bar. This is preferred to graying unselectable menu items.

Pop-up Menus

A *pop-up menu* is a floating menu that can be attached to a portion of the screen or a control. It is very useful for those options which are appropriate to the screen or control, but are not essential for completing the task. In general, the user clicks the right mouse button to bring up the active pop-up menu, if any.

The choices in a pop-up menu should be in the same order as they appear on any other menu. If any menu selection opens a window, then place those options first, followed by a separator bar. Clipboard options, such as **Copy**, **Cut**, and **Paste** would be next, followed by another separator bar. Finally, any choices which are provided as a convenience to the user are listed last. If an option exists to set various object properties (such as confirmation of deletions), this option should always be listed last.

Figure 3.7 shows an example of the pop-up menu attached to Delphi running under Windows 95.

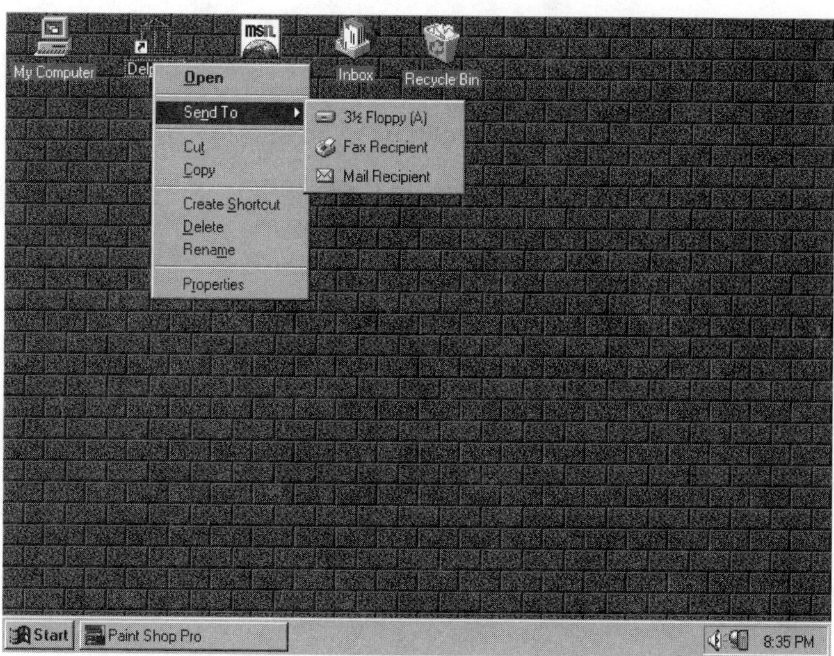

Figure 3.7 Delphi pop-up menu.

Mouse Pointer

The *mouse pointer* is the symbol, usually shaped like an arrow, that is shown on the screen and moved about using the mouse. It primarily aids users in the selection of objects from the window or desktop. However, the pointer can also serve as a visual cue to the user about elements in the system. For example, the hourglass pointer is used to indicate the user needs to wait for some process to complete. The no-drop pointer indicates that the screen object cannot be manipulated by drag and drop operations. For the most part, use the default pointer (of the arrow) should be used, but change the pointer to an hourglass (or other wait pointer) when the user cannot interact with the system until the current process completes. Figure 3.8 shows a few examples of mouse pointers.

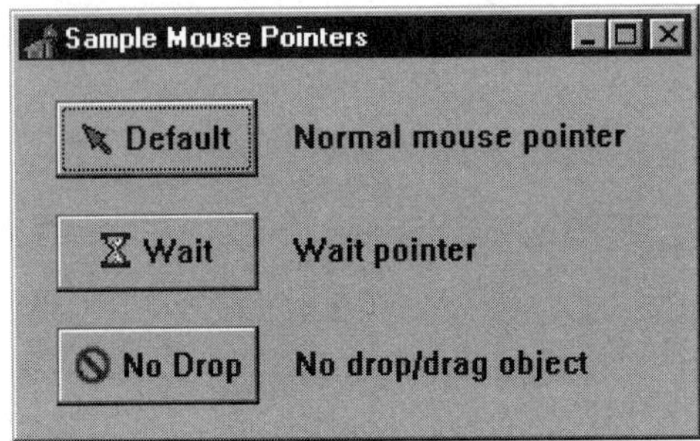

Figure 3.8 Mouse pointer examples.

Text Cursor

The *text cursor* is the visual indication of which control currently has input focus. For the most part, Windows will maintain the text cursor automatically for you. In some applications, the text cursor will change shapes when the user is inserting text as opposed to overwriting text.

Controls

Controls are visual components that allow the user to interact with various data elements. Controls usually have some sort of label attached to or near them to allow the user to move about the window. While these control operate similarly to GETS and SAYS in Xbase languages, one thing to keep in mind is that the user does not have to fill out the control sequentially. The controls should not depend upon completion of a prior control, since you can't guarantee the order in which the user will complete the screen. We will cover controls in much more detail in Chapter 4. In this section, we will only briefly cover the purpose and use of the various CUA controls.

Text Box

A *text box* or *edit* control is used to collect straight text from the user. It is most similar to the @ GET clause from Xbase languages. If you need to get text from the user without providing any choices, such as a name or address, then a text box control is appropriate. Delphi and Visual Basic also provide a concept called edit masks, which are very similar to Xbase's Picture clauses. Social security numbers, zip codes, and postal codes are good candidates for edit masks on text controls.

In cases where longer text is required (over about 60 characters), a text box control is still an option, but it must be specified it as multi-line. Delphi provides a memo control which operates very much like a multi-line edit control.

List Box

A *list box* control is used when the list of possible choices is a predefined number for the user to pick one or more from. When using this control, the user will be able to use the arrow keys to move between choices and the space key to mark the current entry.

When using a list box, choices should be in alphabetic order, or in ascending order for numeric choices. Ideally, six to eight choices should be shown in the list box. The width of the list box should be large enough to display most of the choices; however, it is possible some choices will be truncated or require a horizontal scroll bar.

If screen space is a concern, you can use a drop-down list box control. This variant of the list box does not display the list until the control gets input focus. When this occurs, the user can click the mouse or press the **space** bar to have the list box appear. Once the user selects an item from the box, the item will be displayed and the list box will neatly tuck itself away. Figure 3.9 shows an example of a regular list box and an expanded drop-down list box.

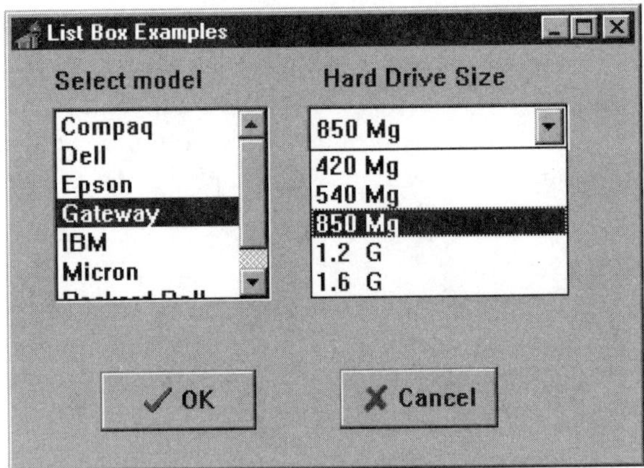

Figure 3.9 List Box control.

Combination Box

A *combination box* control (or combobox for short) is a control that combines the features of an edit box with those of a list box. The user can type a value in the field or optionally select a value from the list box. The value the user enters does not have to be found on the list.

The combobox is best used when some freely entered text is required, but suggested values are offered to the user. Similar to the list box, at least six entries below the edit text or use the drop-down variant if space is lacking on the form. As the user types in the edit box, the list will be positioned at the closest match.

Push Button

The **push button** control is a box containing text and/or graphics which has some sort of action associated with it. In Figure 3.9, the OK and Cancel options are both push buttons. If the user clicks on the button, then the appropriate action will be performed.

You should always include an OK button and a Cancel button on your forms. This allows the user to confirm his changes or cancel them easily. You can also select one push button to serve as the default action. The default button is the one that gets selected if the user merely pushes the **Enter** key. For the most part, this option would be the OK choice, unless the OK choice is destructive. For example, a "format drive C:" option should probably default to **Cancel**, not **OK**.

Radio Buttons

A *radio button* control is used to present a list of mutually exclusive choices and allow the user to select one. Once a choice is checked, the other choices will automatically be unchecked. The control's name comes from older radio models that operated with buttons that would only allow one to be depressed at a time.

Radio buttons are also referred to as option buttons. Figure 3.10 shows an example of a radio button control to select the preferred shipping method, as well as some edit controls and push buttons.

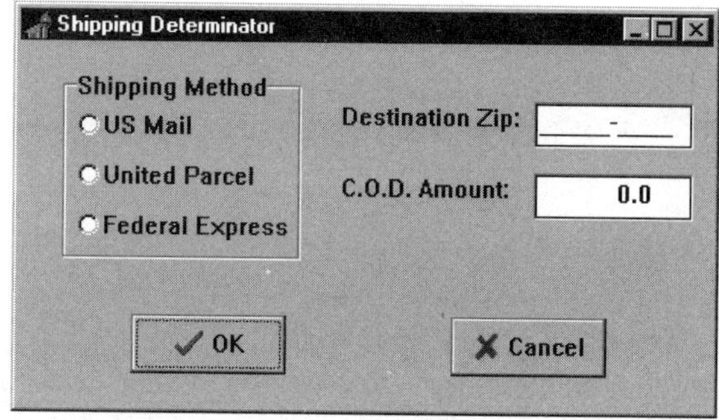

Figure 3.10 Radio Button control.

Check Boxes

A *check box* is a control used to represent a setting or option that has two discreet choices, such as **ON/OFF** or **YES/NO**. The logical data type from Xbase could fit well in a check box control. Checkboxes are frequently in a group to allow multiple settings to be selected. For example, we might want to add check boxes for insurance, required signature, or deliver Saturday to our shipping window in Figure 3.10.

Sliders

A *slider* is a control that represents a particular quantity within a range of values. In multimedia programs, the volume is frequently represented with a slider control. Even though the slider (or taskbar control) is a standard CUA control, it is not present in Delphi (16 bit version) or Visual Basic 3.x. The Windows 95 versions of both products do have slider controls.

Designing the Interface

Once the objects are determined, a determination is made on how to use the CUA components and controls to present these objects to the user. Some objects, such as the account object, should be displayed within the context of their container object, while others, such as the check, can be displayed either within the register object or by itself. For a company with only a few checks, forcing the user to write checks from the checkbook might work well. For a larger company that has periodic check runs, it might make more sense to have an isolated check writing component.

When programming in DOS, a temptation exists to immediately develop a menu structure to provide access to the objects. In Windows however, the menu is often a secondary method of selecting objects. Therefore , the menu does not have to be created. Figure 3.11 shows an example of a Windows program that can easily be understood, yet does not rely on a menu bar at all.

Figure 3.11 Audiostation.

Some Guidelines Towards a Good User Interface

Designing a good user interface is still somewhat of an art-form, regardless of the platform. While the CUA guidelines offer suggestions for most aspects of the interface, it is akin to describing the best way to create each room, while leaving it to the architect to put the rooms together in a way that forms a house. Here are some guidelines to help design a good interface.

Allow the User to Focus on the Task, Not the Software

A good interface should be transparent to the user. It should so closely mimic the process it is doing, that the user forgets he or she is using a computer. Think about the task being accomplished and design the screen to do the minimal amount of work to accomplish it. Do not require any extra steps that the user would not performed by hand. A good example can be found in **Microsoft Money**'s check writing window (see Figure 3.12). It is very focused on the current task, i.e., writing a check.

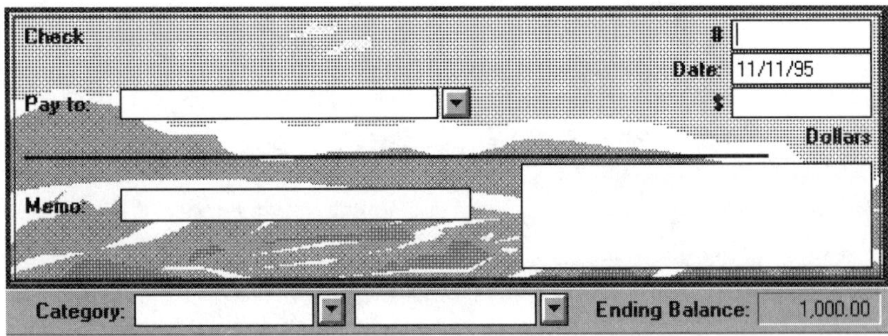

Figure 3.12 Check Writing with Microsoft's Money.

Keep the current task in mind for each screen you design. Eliminate any unnecessary steps and hide any extra options away so they don't interfere with the task at hand.

Also, hide any optional procedure related to the current task. For example, in the check writing example above, the program may allow the user to change the check background or switch the monetary unit from dollars to pounds or francs. Although these tasks should be associated with the check form itself, they are not part of the main task the form is trying to accomplish. You might want to consider use of a pop-up menu to provide access to these features. This way they are easily available, yet still do not distract the user from the main focus of the screen.

Keep the Actions Consistent

The user of your program should get a feeling of comfort whenever they venture into different parts of the application. Take the time to look for similar aspects of your application and make sure they operate the same way. For instance, if two character state abbreviations are used instead of full state names, make sure all state inputs work the same way. If you use radio buttons to select a person's party affiliation, don't use list boxes to get the same information in another part of the application.

Figure 3.13 shows an example of three valid methods to select a shipping method. Any one of the three could be used, but whichever one is used, should be used any time shipping methods are used.

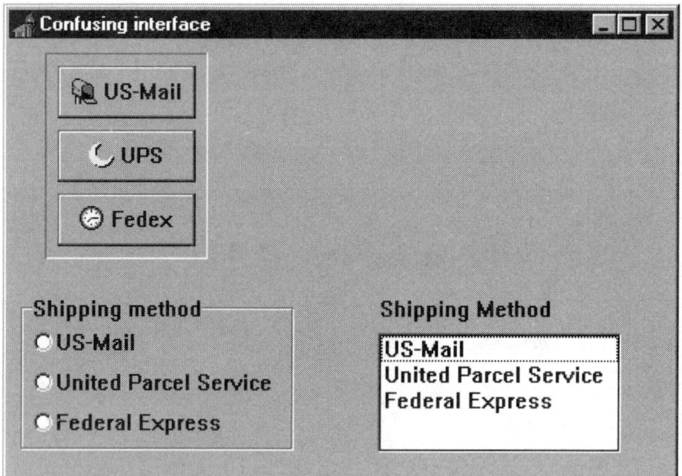

Figure 3.13 Different methods of determining how to ship.

This can be particularly important when programming in a team environment. Decide upon the preferred method to collect or display various data within the system. Users may feel uncomfortable with a shifting interface, although they might not be able to pinpoint quite what's wrong.

Let the User Be in Charge, Not the Software

DOS programmers have strict control over the user, imposing a one-task-at-a-time mentality on them. However, users don't work that way. Frequently the user will need to postpone what they are doing, do something else, and then return to where they were. Windows programming accommodates this multi-task ability of the user quite nicely. A user can minimize a window and switch to do something else or maximize the window to focus only on it.

This minimize/maximize ability should not just be limited to the main form. Rather, it should be a consistent part of the application. Imagine an order-entry form that allows new orders to be recorded. If the user has the customer on the telephone, she might want to stop taking the order to fill out the customer profile form, and then return back to the order.

Although the user should have the freedom to use your system any way they want, there may be times that your program needs to force a response from the user before proceeding. For example, Figure 3.14 shows a dialog box encountered when the printer is not responding.

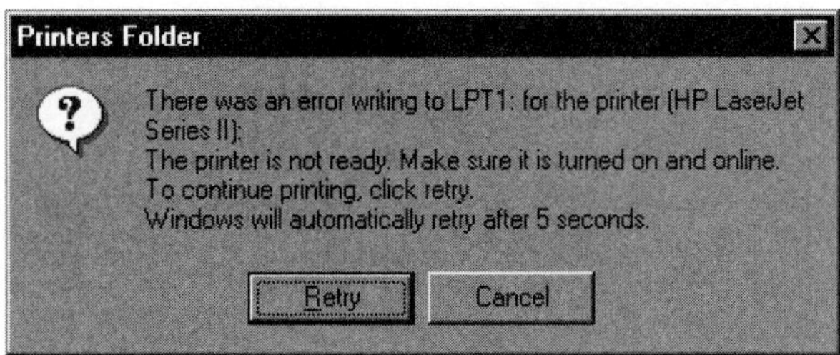

Figure 3.14 Modal printer error dialog.

This dialog box has no minimize box and the user's only options are to fix the printer and retry or to cancel the print job. The application is telling the user that it cannot proceed until the user addresses the problem. Situations such as printer error or irreversible procedures should require an answer from the user and not allow the user to minimize the dialog box.

Provide Immediate Feedback

Once the user makes a choice, the software should immediately show the impact of that choice or if not feasible, at least some indication that the choice was received by the software. The user should not have to wait for some additional process before they can gauge the impact of the change. If the user changes fonts, the new font should be immediately shown. If they select bold face, the marked text should be immediately bolded.

If it is not possible to immediately show the impact of the change, at least show some indication that the command was received. For example, Figure 3.15 shows a progression of envelope icons from Intuit's Quicken Expensable program. As the user clicks on the **submitted** button, the envelope closes. As soon the expense report is paid, the PAID sticker appears on the envelope. This example illustrates a good method of providing visible feedback to the user as he or she clicks a button.

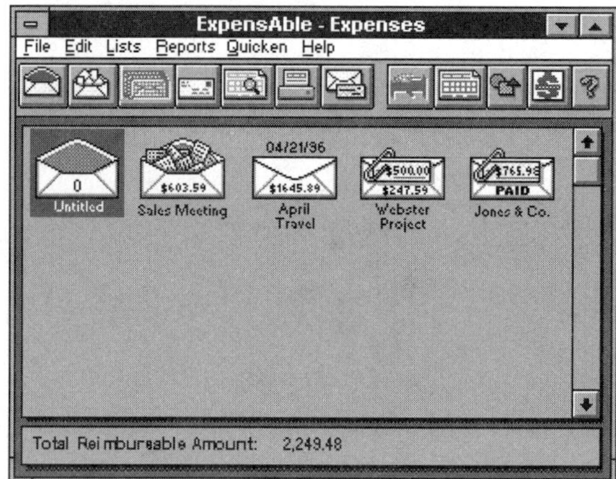

Figure 3.15 Envelope icons from Intuit's Expensable.

Make it Difficult to Damage and Easy to Repair

When presenting options for the user, always make the safest choice the easiest to select. For example, if the program wants to overwrite an existing file on a disk, the user's choices would be to:

Overwrite the file: This could potentially destroy quite a bit of work. Imagine the novice user who loads the Excel payroll spreadsheet and saves it as a Word document.

Cancel the save request: Of course, not saving the work at all could be just as disastrous (which is why most programs remind the user to save work before they exit the application).

Choose a different file name: This is the least destructive choice of the three, so it should probably be the default action.

However, you should balance user convenience with data protection. If the file the user wants to overwrite is the file they initially loaded, then probably overwriting the existing file would be a more logical default. If your application can determine that the type of file to be overwritten is not the kind your application creates, you should probably provide additional warnings before overwriting the file.

Figure 3.16 shows an example of a warning message if the user is about to format a disk drive. Notice that the first action is to not format the drive, and the user has to specifically move and select the push button if they want to format the drive. There is no accelerator key attached to the destructive choice. It is also very clear what answering Yes or No means in this message.

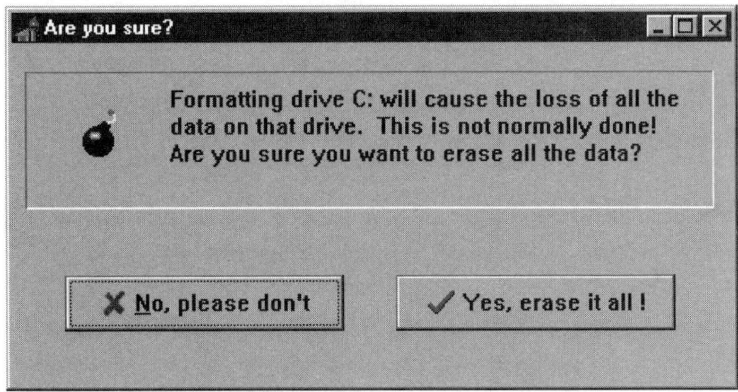

Figure 3.16 Example warning message.

It is just as important to make it easy to repair damage or undo erroneous choices. Although this requires some additional coding—such as making a backup copy of the overwritten file—it installs a confidence in the user to work with your software. Take the time to consider how the software can recover from potential problems. Adding such a safety net will make the software much more robust and users will feel more comfortable with your program.

Reduce How Much the User Needs to Remember

The user should not have to remember something that the computer program can remember for him or her. People are much better at recognition rather than recall, so wherever possible, the software should present lists to the user to select an option.

Your program should remember the last file the user was working with so the user can easily pick the file. The Most Recently Used ("MRU") list in most word processing and spreadsheet programs is an example of allowing the user to select from a list rather than have to remember a file name. You might also fill in the last price paid when a user enters an item number, or the last amount a check was written for to a particular vendor.

Summary

CUA offers suggestions for the various components that make up a user interface. It is your job as application designer to try to determine a proper mix and structure of these components to produce an attractive user interface. Perhaps the best way to get comfortable developing interfaces is to explore existing software packages. Get a feel for which components and operations you, and more importantly, your users, feel comfortable working with.

CHAPTER 4:

THE FORM IN DETAIL

In the first few chapters, we've discussed the form and how to place a menu on it. We also covered how to tweak some of the form's behaviors by adjusting property values. In this chapter, we will cover the form in depth, and show how you can attach the CUA controls discussed in chapter three to your forms to create an application.

The Form

Each program you write will have a main form (i.e., the first one you work on when you enter Delphi or Visual Basic) that is your application's driver program. All actions and subsequent forms will flow from this starting point. Figure 4.1 shows the main form generated by Visual Basic.

Figure 4.1 Main Form.

When your program starts, the main form gains control and the user may interact with it. The main form can generate other forms or everything you need to accomplish might be done on the same form.

Working with Multiple Forms

Applications will frequently create additional forms to work with. There are several form styles that you can use depending upon the needs of your application.

Single Document Interface

The Single Document Interface (SDI) is an interface style in which all interaction with the program is accomplished in a primary window with a number of ancillary windows. This is probably the style you are most familiar with from DOS programming. In many DOS applications, there is a primary screen with a main menu attached. Each menu option brings up a secondary form to collect information from the user.

The default form style in both Visual Basic and Delphi is for SDI forms. For most of our accounting application, we will use the SDI form style.

Delphi and Visual Basic are both examples of SDI applications. For example, Figure 4.2 shows the primary window in Delphi.

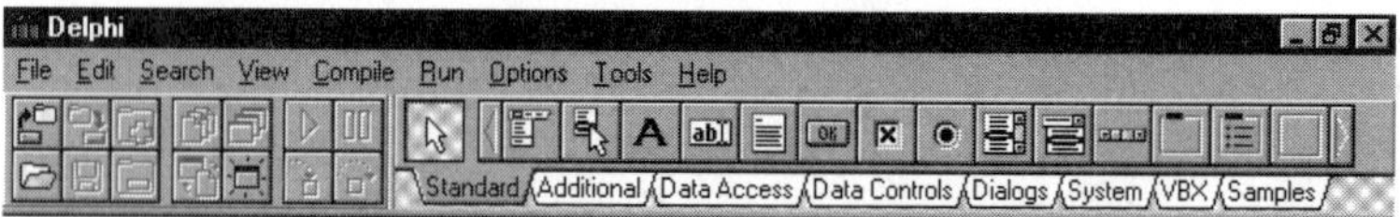

Figure 4.2 Delphi's primary window.

The form consists of a title bar, a menu bar, and a series of buttons that are grouped into the speedbar and component palette. As you work with the menu and/or buttons, you can create secondary windows for Delphi. Figure 4.3 shows Delphi with a few of its secondary windows opened.

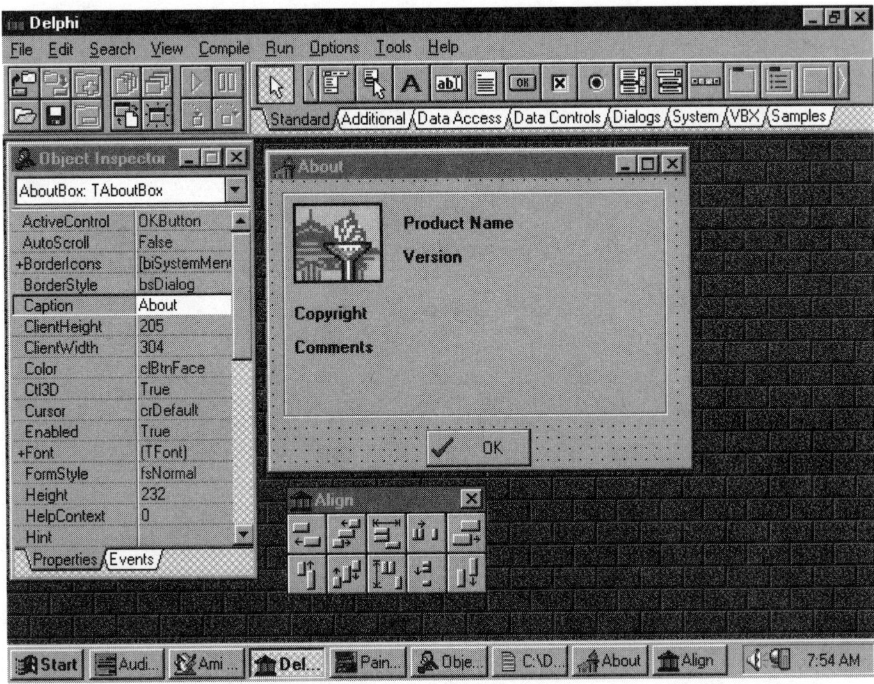

Figure 4.3 Delphi with open secondary windows.

Multiple Document Interface

The Multiple Document Interface (MDI) is an interface style in which a primary window (called the *parent window*) contains a set of related secondary windows (called the *child windows*). Most word processors and spreadsheets provide examples of the MDI style. The program can open multiple files (documents or spreadsheets) each of which is contained within a window. All of the windows are contained by the primary window. Figure 4.4 shows an example MDI application.

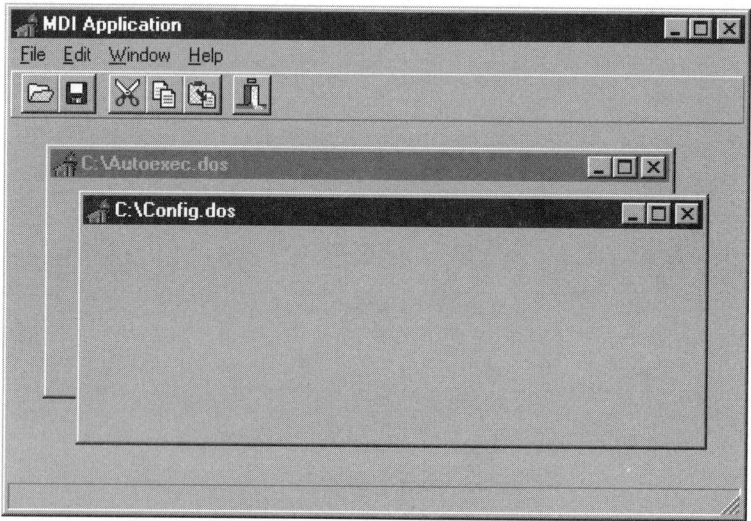

Figure 4.4 Example MDI application.

To create an MDI application, two forms must be created, the parent form (called the MDIform) and the child forms (called MDIchild forms). In Visual Basic, the parent form is a special type of form that you must insert from the menu. In Delphi, you need to change the form's *formstyle* property to fsMDIform. Once the parent form is created, you can create subsequent child forms. The MDI parent form has additional methods such as *Tile*, *Cascade*, and *Arrange* which allow the form to control its child forms.

If you have an application that allows similar operations on any number of forms, you should consider using the MDI style. For purpose of this book, however, we will primarily be working with the SDI style since it is the most similar to DOS programming.

Tabbed Notebooks

Another style of application is the tabbed notebooks (also called the workbook). Tabbed notebooks are useful for programs that have different types of form dialogs that need to be placed together under a containing form. Figure 4.5 shows an example of a tabbed notebook taken from Delphi's project options.

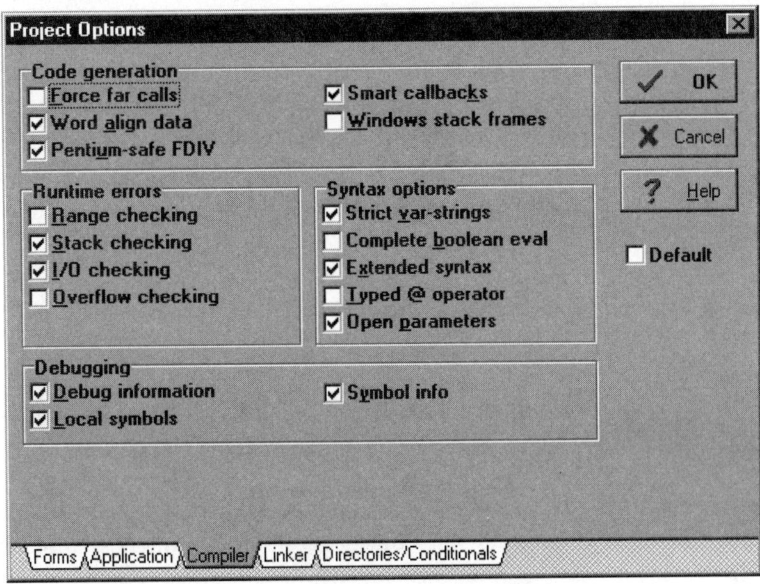

Figure 4.5 Tabbed notebook example.

The user can flip between pages by selecting the appropriate tab. Each tab has a different screen associated with it, yet all screens are related.

Selecting a Style

No one style is appropriate for all situations. You need to consider the object you are modelling and how its data is related. The SDI style is appropriate if your application manages several different types of data, each with little relation to one another. This is typical of our DOS applications, where a menu ties together various screens, each independent of the other.

The MDI style is an appropriate when you need to manage multiple occurences of similar data, such as when editing multiple files or E-mail. The tabbed notebook style is good when you have different views or object types that are related. It provides easy navigation between the views, however, it makes it difficult to look at two views simultaneously.

Form Properties

Each form you create, regardless of the style, will be controlled by a number of properties and methods. A property is similar to a variable in XBASE, except that it is restricted in scope to the appropriate form. A method is similar to a function, because it is restricted to operating within the form.

All forms have a large number of properties that affect the form and how it operates. We will discuss some of the more common ones here.

Name

Every form must have a *name*, which is how your program code will refer to the form. The name must be a unique identifier that contain numbers, characters, and underscores, but it must not start with a number. In Delphi, the name can be up to 63 characters. In Visual Basic the name cannot be more than 40 characters.

Form names are defined when your are designing your program (called design time), and they cannot be changed while your program is running (run-time).

Caption

The *caption* property contains the text that appears in the form's title bar. You can access it both at design time and at run-time. For example, you might use the caption 'Chart of Accounts:' at design time, and at run-time, add the current account number being edited to the caption text.

Top and Left

The *top* and *left* properties determine where the form is placed on the desktop. You normally would not directly work with these properties because drawing the form and moving it around updates these values. In Delphi, screen locations and size are expressed in pixels. Pixel is short for '*picture element*' and represents the smallest unit of measurement on the screen. In Visual Basic, the location and size are specified by the current unit scale of the form. The *scalemode* property on a Visual Basic form, which can be pixels, characters, inches, etc.

Height and Width

The *height* and *width* properties determine the size of the form. As with *top* and *left*, you normally would not directly work with these properties.

ClientHeight and ClientWidth

Each form has two areas in it. One is the frame and title bar which are the areas controlled by Windows. The other area is the client area, which is the area that your application program uses. The *ClientHeight* and *ClientWidth* properties are similar to *height* and *width*, but only for the client portion of the form.

Visible

In order for the user to interact with the form, it must be *visible*. However, even if this boolean value is **false**, your program can still work with the form's properties and methods. For example, an order form may also contain a shipping form which would initially be invisible. When the user is ready to complete the order, the shipping form would be made visible so the user could fill out the appropriate information.

ActiveControl

The *ActiveControl* property references the control that currently has focus, or has focus initially when the form loads. Your program can use the ActiveControl property to access properties and methods of the active control. Only the active control, can have focus at a given time in an application.

Cursor/MousePointer

The *Cursor* (Delphi) or *MousePointer* (Visual Basic) property is the image used when the mouse moves onto the form. For most applications, you will use the default cursor; however, if your form is performing a process that prevents the user from interacting with the form, then you should switch the cursor to the hourglass shape.

Ctl3d (Delphi) /Appearance (Visual Basic)

This property determines whether the window should have a three-dimensional appearance. In Delphi, set*Ctl3D* to a TRUE value if you want to have a three-dimensional, sculpted appearance to the form. If set to FALSE, the control has a two-dimensional appearance. In Visual Basic, set *Appearance* to 1-3D to enable three-dimensional effects, or 0-Flat to disable them.

Icon

The *icon* property indicates which graphic bitmap file should be used to represent the window when it is minimized. While there is no counterpart to the icon in DOS programming, icons and graphic representations of objects are standard in Windows programming.

WindowState

The *WindowState* property determines the initial state of the form. In DOS programming, we are used to designing for the entire screen, but this is not typical of Windows programming. These are the possible values:

Delphi Value	Visual Basic Value	Meaning
wsNormal	0-Normal	The form appears as it was designed (this is the default)
wsMinimized	1-Minimized	The form is minimized (shown as an icon)
wsMaximized	2-Maximized	The form is maximized (occupies the full screen)

Tag

The *tag* property is specifically designed for the programmer. Delphi and Visual Basic both provide the property, but do not make any use of it. Tag allows the programmer to attach a value and carry it around with the form. You can use this property just the same as any other property. In Delphi, the tag property is a numeric value. In Visual Basic, this property is a string value.

Form Methods

While the properties determine how the form behaves, the methods cause the form to do something with those properties and to interact with the user.

Show

The *Show* method makes the form visible by setting its Visible property to TRUE. If the form is obscured when the method is called, Show tries to make the form visible by bringing it to the front with the *BringToFront / Zorder(0)* method.

Close / Unload

The *Close* method (Delphi) / *Unload* <form> command (Visual Basic) closes a form. Closing the form corresponds to the user selecting the **Close** menu item on the form's System menu. The code attached to the OnClose event will be executed.

BringToFront/ Zorder(0)

The *BringToFront* method (Delphi) / *Zorder(0)* function (Visual Basic) puts the form in front of all other forms on the desktop. The order in which forms are stacked on top of each other is called the Z order (hence the Visual Basic function name).

SendToBack/ Zorder(1)

The *SendToBack* method (Delphi) or *Zorder(1)* function (Visual Basic) puts the form behind the other forms on the desktop.

Hide

The *Hide* method makes the form invisible by setting the *Visible* property of the form to False. A form that is hidden is not visible and the user cannot access any of its controls. Your program code, however, can still set the properties of the form or call any of its methods.

Refresh

The *Refresh* method erases whatever is currently on the form and then repaints the entire form by calling the form's repaint procedure.

Form Events

Another equally important component of form design are the events. Events tell your program when the code you write should be executed. In a DOS program, you need to write code that decides when the code is performed, as well as writing the code itself. Under Windows, though, Windows will decide when code should be executed. All that needs to be written is the code to be performed and then specify what event needs to happen for the code to be performed.

OnCreate/Load

The *OnCreate* (Delphi)/*Load* (Visual Basic) event occurs when Windows first creates a form. For the main form, this usually occurs during program startup. Secondary forms are created with the *Create* method. This is a good time to attach any initialization code you need to have accomplished. For example, you might have a standard list of strings to attached to a list box when the form starts or you might want to enable/disable various controls depending upon some condition when the form is created.

OnActivate/Activate

The *OnActivate* (Delphi) /*Activate* (Visual Basic) event occurs when the form becomes active. A form becomes active when focus is transferred to it. This occurs when the user clicks on the form, or if the form's show method is called.

In Visual Basic, there is also a *GotFocus* event which occurs when focus is moved to the form. In Visual Basic, the code attached to the Activate event is executed first, followed by the code associated with the GotFocus event.

OnClick/Click

The *OnClick* (Delphi)/*Click* (Visual Basic) event gets called whenever the user clicks on the form itself (not one of the form's controls). While this event is available for forms, it is more useful on controls and menu items which are discussed shortly.

OnDblClk /DblClick

The *OnClick* (Delphi)/*Click* (Visual Basic) event gets called whenever the user double-clicks on the form itself (not one of the form's controls). As with the Click event, this event is more useful on controls rather than forms.

OnClose/UnLoad

The *OnClose* (Delphi) /*Unload* (Visual Basic) event specifies which event handler to call when a form is about to close. The handler specified by OnClose might, for example, test to make sure all fields in a data-entry form have valid contents before allowing the form to close.

A form is closed by the Close method or when the user chooses Close from the form's system menu. In Delphi, the OnClose event gets sent a parameter which determines the action. Your code can set this parameter to one of the following values:

Value	Meaning
caNone	The form is not allowed to close, so nothing happens.
caHide	The form just hidden. Your program can still access a hidden form.
caFree	The form is closed and all allocated memory for the form is freed.
caMinimize	The form is minimized, rather than closed.

In Visual Basic, a numeric parameter is passed to the function. If you set this argument to any nonzero value, it prevents the form from being removed.

OnCloseQuery/QueryUnload

The *OnCloseQuery* (Delphi)/*QueryUnload* (Visual Basic) event occurs when the form is about to close (such as the close method being called or the user selecting Close from the system menu). An OnCloseQuery event handler contains a Boolean variable that determines whether a form is allowed to close. Its default value is True.

You can use an OnCloseQuery event handler to ask users if they are sure they want the form closed immediately. If the user wants to shut down Windows while your application is running, this event will be called.

OnDestroy/Terminate

The *OnDestroy* (Delphi) / *Terminate* (Visual Basic) event occurs when a form is about to be destroyed. A form is destroyed by the Destroy, Free, or Release methods, or when the main form of the application is closed.

In Visual Basic, the *Terminate* event code is performed after any code is attached to the *Unload* event.

OnDeactivate/Deactivate

The *OnDeactivate* (Delphi) /*Deactivate* (Visual Basic) event occurs when the user switches from one application to another Windows application. The OnDeactive event is used to do any special processing before your application is deactivated.

In Visual Basic, the *Deactivate* event code is performed after any code is attached to the *LostFocus* event.

OnPaint/Paint

The *OnPaint* (Delphi)/ *Paint* (Visual Basic) event occurs when Windows requires the form to redraw itself (called painting). Windows keeps track of the visibility and focus of forms. If a form becomes visible and was covered by others forms, then Windows will send a paint request to the form to ensure its appearance is up to date.

It is not necessary to redraw any controls attached to the form during a repaint event because they are done automatically. However, if you have any graphics output on the form, you will need to repaint that output.

OnResize/Resize

The *OnResize* (Delphi) /*Resize* (Visual Basic) event occurs whenever the form is resized while an application is running. Use the OnResize event handler when you want something to happen in your application when the form is resized.

While writing code to handle resizing of all components on a form is a complex undertaking, you might need to resize a multiline edit component to display more lines of text if the user increases the form size. This would be done by adjusting the height property of the control. For example, you would make sure the height property is always 100 pixels less than the form's height. If the form's height is increased, then the multiline edit component's height property is increased as well.

OnShow/GotFocus

The *OnShow* (Delphi) / *GotFocus* (Visual Basic) event's code gets called whenever the form becomes the active form. Note that this event occurs just before a form becomes visible.

Attaching Code to Events

Once you've decided upon the code to execute and the event to attach it to, you merely need to hook the two together. In Delphi, this is accomplished by using the object inspector, which lists the various events for each component in a tab, much like the property variables. Figure 4.6 shows the events for the form component.

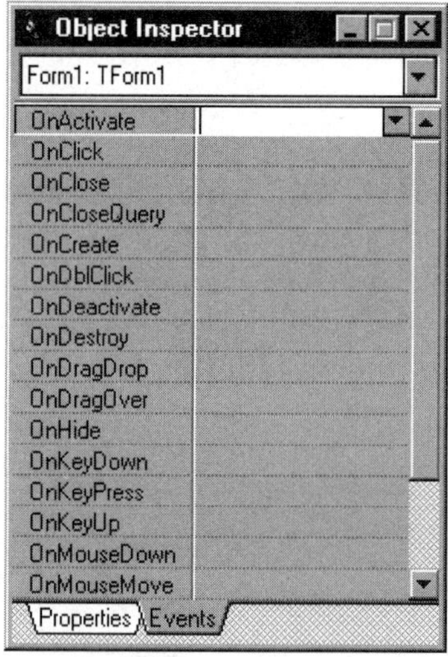

Figure 4.6 Form events in Delphi's object inspector.

To attach code, you find the event in the list and double click on it. This will bring up the code window as shown in Figure 4.7.

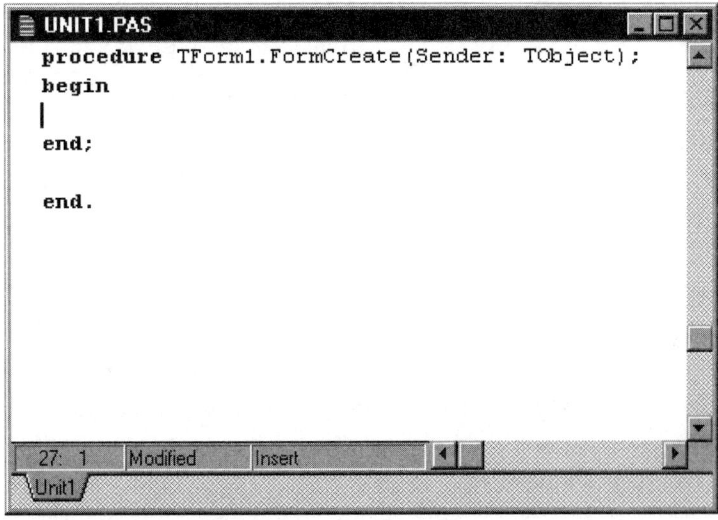

Figure 4.7 Delphi's code editor window.

In Visual Basic, you need to either double click on the form or press the F7 function key. Either method will bring up the Visual Basic code editor window, shown in Figure 4.8.

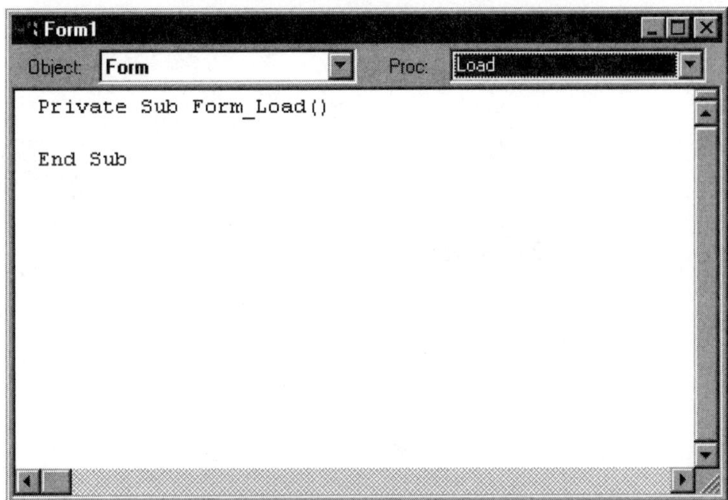

Figure 4.8 Visual Basic code editor.

By clicking on the drop down listbox titled **Proc:**, you can bring up a list of events. Visual Basic will create an appropriate function name and allow you to write code for that event.

What Kind of Code?

Now that we've found out where the code resides, we need to review what kind of code we can write here. However, since this book is not a primer on any particular programming language (either Visual Basic or Delphi), we are not going to go into much detail about the code.

You can essentially write any code you'd like, subject to the language's syntax. The most common use of this section, however, will be to set property values of controls and/or to perform the events associated with the form or control.

For example, you probably should include some sort of command button on your main form to close the application. Listing 4.1 shows what type code might look like in Visual Basic and Listing 4.2 shows the Delphi code to close the main form (and hence the application). Note that Visual Basic and Delphi automatically generate the procedure names and structure, you merely need to add the code between the procedure and the end clause.

Listing 4.1 Visual Basic code to close the application.

```
Private Sub CloseButton_Click()
    Unload MainForm
    End
End Sub
```

Listing 4.2 Delphi code to close the main form (hence the application).

```
procedure TMainForm.CloseButtonBtnClick(Sender: TObject);
begin
     close ;
end;
```

Later in the chapter we will have a number of examples from our accounting program showing various code elements of both languages. In addition, Appendix A review's some Xbase coding constructs and shows their Delphi and Visual Basic counterparts.

Attaching Controls to Forms

Controls are the primary means by which users interact with the program's data. In Delphi and Visual Basic, controls are placed on the form by selecting the desired control from the toolbox and dragging it onto the form. Figure 4.9 shows Visual Basic's toolbox and Figure 4.10 shows Delphi's toolbar.

Figure 4.9 Visual Basic's toolbox (standard edition).

Figure 4.10 Delphi's toolbar (standard toolbar only).

To work with either toolbar, you merely click the mouse on the icon that represents the control and then click on the form. This will create a new control on the form which you can then manipulate.

Common Properties

Controls share some common properties, regardless of the type of control. These properties are described here.

Name

Every control on a form must have a name. This name is how the form and other controls communicate with the control. The control name must be a unique identifier containing numbers, characters, and underscores. It must not start with a number. In Delphi, the name can be up to 63 characters while in Visual Basic, the name cannot be more than 40 characters.

Although default control names will be created unless you like using Edit1 or CheckBox2, you should assign meaningful names to your controls to make your code more readable. Which code is more readable?

```
if edit6.text = "USA"  then edit6.editmask = "#####"
```

or

```
if country.text = "USA" then zipcode.editmask = "#####"
```

Control names are defined when your are designing your program (appropriately called design time) and they cannot be changed while your program is running (run-time).

Caption/Text

The *Caption* property (or *Text* property in the Delphi edit controls) contains the actual string data that the user can edit

Top and Left

The *Top* and *Left* properties determine where the control is placed on the form. You normally would not directly work with these properties since placing the control on the form and moving it around updates these values. In Delphi, screen location and size are expressed in pixels. In Visual Basic, the location and size are specified by the current unit scale of the form. (The *scalemode* property on a Visual Basic form, which can be pixels, characters, inches, etc.).

Height and Width

The *Height* and *Width* properties determine the size of the control on the form. As with top and left, you normally would not directly work with these properties.

Enabled

Enabled is boolean property which determines whether or not this control can receive input focus. The user may only interact with the current control.

Visible

Visible is a boolean property that determines whether or not the control appears on the screen and can be seen by the user. You might use this property if you have control that only is appropriate if a certain value is entered in a different control.

Font

The *Font* property is a font object that controls the attributes of text written on or in the component. In Delphi, to modify a font, you change the value of the Color, Name, Size, or Style properties of the font object. In Visual Basic, the standard font dialog window appears if you want to modify a control's font.

Cursor/MousePointer

The *Cursor* (Delphi) / *MousePointer* (Visual Basic) property allows you to control the shape of the mouse cursor when it enters a particular control.

TabStop

The *Tabstop* property is a boolean value that indicates if the user can tab into this control. For label controls, tabstop defaults to False. For most other controls, its value is True.

Taborder/Tabindex

The *Taborder* (Delphi)/*Tabindex* (Visual Basic) property is a numeric value that determines the sequence that the controls will be traversed. By default, the program will assign the sequence numbers in the same order as you put them on the form at design time. You can, however, change the sequence at both design time and run-time.

Borderstyle

The *BorderStyle* property of edit boxes, list boxes, memo controls, grid controls, outlines, and scroll boxes determines whether these components have a border. These are the possible values:

Delphi	Visual Basic	Meaning
bsNone	0-None	No visible border
bsSingle	1-Fixed Single	Single-line border

Ctl3D /Appearance

The *Ctl3D* (Delphi) / *Appearance* (Visual Basic) property determines how the control appears. In Delphi, if Ctl3D contains a TRUE value the form will have a three-dimensional, sculpted appearance. If set to FALSE, the control will have two-dimensional appearance. In Visual Basic, set Appearance to 1-3D to enable three-dimensional effects, or 0-Flat to disable them.

Tag

The *tag* property is a user-defined property created for whatever you would like to place in it. The property value is numeric in Delphi and character in Visual Basic.

Common Methods and Events

In addition to properties, there are some common methods and events shared by most controls. You will not often need to use methods with controls because the control does all of the necessary work to manipulate the control's value. However, just as you use events to attach code to your form, you will also use events to attach code to controls. The most common events will be the Click and the Keypress events.

OnChange/Change Event

The *OnChange* (Delphi) / *Change* (Visual Basic) event occurs prior to when a new control is selected (the TabIndex value is about to change). This event code can coordinate data display among controls. For example, you might want to update a text box's value when the attached slider is changed, or display data and formulas in one control and the results in another.

OnClick/Click Event

The *OnClick* (Delphi) / *Click* (Visual Basic) event occurs when the user clicks the mouse button while the mouse pointer is over the component. For radio buttons and check boxes, this action also causes the control value to be updated.

OnDblClick Event

The *OnDblClick* (Delphi) / *DblClick* (Visual Basic) event occurs when the user double clicks the mouse button while the mouse pointer is over the component.

OnEnter/GotFocus Event

The *OnEnter* (Delphi) / *GotFocus* (Visual Basic) event occurs when a control becomes active. Use this event handler to specify any special processing you want to occur when the control becomes active.

OnExit /LostFocus Event

The *OnExit* (Delphi) /*LostFocus* (Visual Basic) event occurs when the input focus shifts away from one control to another. Use this event handler when you want special processing to occur when this control ceases to be active. This is particularly useful for data validations on the contents of the control.

OnKeyDown/Keydown Event

The *OnKeyDown* (Delphi) / *Keydown* (Visual Basic) event occurs when a user presses any key while the control has focus. This event can check for any special keypress you want to handle within the control.

In Visual Basic, the key code and shift status are both passed into the function as integers. The key code is one of a number of constants to indentify the key (the *vbKey* code constants). The shift status is a number with bits representing **shift** (1), **control** (2), and **alt** (4). If the user were to press **Control Shift** and **Enter** in the control, the keycode would contain *vbKeyReturn* and the shift status would contain 3 (1 shift + 2 control).

In Delphi, the function receives an integer representing the key that was pressed and a shiftstate object. The shiftstate object is a set containing any number of the following values, *ssShift*, *ssAlt*, and/or *ssCtrl*.

Command Button

The first control we will look at is the *Command button*. The Command button, which is also called a Pushbutton, is a control that generally has some code associated with it, usually attached to the *click* event. This attached code will be executed when the user clicks on the button.

Command Button Properties

In addition to the properties used by all controls, the Command Button also has two additional properties of interest. Both properties are boolean (logical) values which determine if the command button should be the default or cancel button for the form.

Default Property

The Command Button specified as the *Default* contains the code that gets executed when the user presses **Enter** on the form. There can only be one Default Command Button per form. You can set this property value to TRUE to make the button the default action.

Cancel Property

The *Cancel* Command Button contains the code that gets executed when the user presses **Esc** on the form. There can only be one Cancel Command Button per form. You can set this property value to TRUE to make this command button the cancel action for the form.

Using Command Buttons

Once you've created a button, you need to attach code to one of the buttons event handlers. Although there are a number of events associated with the button control, the most commonly used is the *Click* event. You should provide your user with an OK or Close button which saves whatever work was done on the form and a Cancel button, which aborts the changes. You should always make the least destructive Pushbutton the default. This is generally the OK button, but for an option such as formatting the disk, Cancel would be a better default choice.

In addition to the regular Command Button, Delphi also has a component called the BitBtn (Bitmap Button) which operate similarly to Command Buttons, but also contains a small bitmap image in addition to the button's caption text. These buttons also have a Kind property which provides a quick way to create standard buttons such as OK and Close.

Label Controls

The Label Control is the Windows counterpart to the Xbase @ SAY command. It is used to put literal text onto the form. The actual text is stored in the caption property, which can be accessed both at design time and run-time. The top and left pixels are similar to the row and column coordinates from the @ SAY command.

Label Properties

In addition to the standard control properties, the Label Control has a few more properties that impact its appearance on the screen.

AutoSize Property

The *AutoSize* property is a logical value that determines if the label size changes to accommodate the width and length of its text. If AutoSize is TRUE (the default in Delphi, but not in Visual Basic), then the label's size will be adjusted. Font changes will also resize the label if AutoSize is enabled.

Alignment

The *Alignment* property determines how the text is justified within the label. In Visual Basic, the property values are:

0- left justify

1- right justify

2- center

In Delphi, the values are *taLeftJustify*, *taCenter*, and *taRightJustify*. The default for both languages is left justification.

BackStyle/Transparent

The *Backstyle* (Visual Basic) / *Transparent* (Delphi) property determines how the label text is written on the form. If set to transparent (0 in Visual Basic or True in Delphi), then the text is written on top of the background without obscuring it. If set to opaque (1 in Visual Basic or False in Delphi), the text control's background color property fill, the control and overwrites any color or graphics behind it.

The default is opaque, however, if you want to place a label on top of a graphic or image, you should set the label to transparent.

WordWrap

The *Wordwrap* property determines if the text will wrap in the box or be truncated at the right margin. The default value is false.

Edit Box Controls

The Edit Box (or Text Box) control is the Windows counterpart to the Xbase @ GET command. It is used to get straight text from the user. When the control is active, the user can enter text directly into the control. The user's input will be stored in the text property, so your program can access it and perform any desired actions.

Edit Box Properties

In addition to the standard control properties, the Edit Box control has a few more properties that impact its appearance on the screen and how the user can interact with it.

CharCase

The *CharCase* property (in Delphi only) determines the case of the text that the user enters in the edit box. These are the possible values:

Value	Meaning
ecLowerCase	Use only lowercase
ecNormal	Leave case as entered, the default value
ecUpperCase	Force all text to uppercase

If the user tries to enter a different case than the current value of CharCase, the characters the user enters appear in the case specified by CharCase. This is similar to using the @! picture function in Xbase, although there is no picture function which forces lower case in Xbase.

There is no CharCase property in Visual Basic, although you can easily use the UCase() and LCase() functions to convert the text to the desired case

MaxLength

The *MaxLength* property specifies the maximum number of characters the user can enter in an edit box, memo, or combo box. The default setting for MaxLength is 0, which means that there is no limit on the number of characters the control can contain. Any other number limits the number of characters the control will accept.

PasswordChar

The *PasswordChar* property allows you create an Edit Box that displays special characters in place of the entered text. By default, PasswordChar is the null character meaning that the control displays its text as entered. If you specify a Password Character, the control displays that character in place of each character in the control's text.

OEMConvert

The *OEMConvert* property (Delphi only) determines whether the text in the control is converted to OEM characters. If True, the text is converted. If False, which is the default, the characters remain as ANSI characters.

ANSI vs ASCII can cause some confusion when you first work in Windows. Windows use the ANSI standard character set, which is different from the ASCII set of characters in most DOS applications (including DBF files). Although many of the numeric codes are the same, some of the higher numbers have different values. If you store information in a file that a DOS program will be using, then be sure to set OEMConvert to True or convert the data before writing it to the file.

Modified/DataChanged

The *Modified* (Delphi) / *DataChanged* (Visual Basic) property is only available at run-time. It determines whether the text of an Edit Box has changed since it was created or updated. If Modified is True, the text was changed, if False, the text was not changed.

Readonly

The *Readonly* property in Delphi is a boolean property that determines if the edit box is read-only (True) or editable (False). The default value is False, which is good, otherwise editing could be difficult.

Multi-line

The *Multi-line* property, which is only available in Visual Basic, determines if the text will wrap in the box and allow the user to enter more than a single line of text. The default value is False. Delphi has a separate control, the memo control, that provides the same functionality as setting Multi-line to True in Visual Basic.

Manipulating Text at Run Time

In addition to the properties mentioned above, there are additional properties and methods that allow you to manipulate the text at run time. You can access these methods whenever the control gets or loses focus, as well as every time a key is pressed in the control.

Run-Time Properties

You can access various parts of the text in the control by using the *SelStart*, *SelText*, and *SelLength* properties. The SelStart property is the numeric offset into the text string while SelLength is the length of the select portion. SelText returns just the selected portion of the string, while the *Text* property returns the entire string.

Run-Time Methods in Delphi

The *Clear* method clears the entire text value while *Clearselection* clears just the selected portion of the text. You can also interact with the Windows' clipboard using the following methods.

CopyToClipboard copies the selected text selected to the Clipboard and replaces any text that exists there. If no text is selected, nothing is copied.

CutToClipboard deletes the selected text, copies it to the Clipboard, and replaces any text that exists there.

PasteFromClipboard copies the contents of the Clipboard to the control and inserts the contents where the cursor is positioned.

Masked Edit

One of the missing elements of the textbox control in Windows is the picture clause from Xbase. However, Delphi and Visual Basic both have a masked edit control (although it is not available in the standard version of Visual Basic). The masked edit control operates just like the text Edit Box, with the addition of an edit mask (or picture clause in Xbase terminology).

The *Editmask* property contains the picture clause to apply to the text being entered in the control. Table 4.1 shows the various components of the editmask compared with the Xbase counterparts in the picture clause.

Table 4.1 Picture clause versus edit mask

Xbase picture clause	Visual Basic edit character	Delphi edit character
9-numeric only	#-numeric only	#-numeric only
A-alphabetic only	?-alphabetic only	L-alphabetic only
!-upper case	None	> - following chars are upper
N-Alphanumeric	A-Alphanumeric	A-alphanumeric
X-Any character	&-Any ANSI character	a-any character at all
#-Digits, sign, space	#-numeric values	9-digits, sign, and space

When you are working with editmasks, be sure to review the allowed input, as the characters are not the same as their Xbase counterparts.

Xbase versus Windows Labels and Edit Box Controls

Let's compare a small sample of Xbase @ Say / Get commands and their counterparts in Windows. Listing 4.3 shows some Xbase code to display some prompts on the screen and get some data from the user.

Listing 4.3 Some @ says and @ gets.

```
private cCode,cName,nAmt
cCode = space(8)
cName = space(40)
nAmt  = 0

@ 5,10 say "Id code: " get cCode  picture "!!!!!!!!"
@ 6,10 say "Company: " get cName
@ 7,10 say "Balance: " get nAmt   picture "9999.99"

read
```

This code would be reflected with the following controls placed on a form.

Control	Property	Value
label_1	caption	'Id code:'
label_2	caption	'Company:'
label_3	caption	'Balance:'
textBox1	text	' '
	maxlength	8
	charcase	ecUpperCase
textBox2	text	'...40 spaces...'
	maxlength	40
maskedEdit	editmask	#####.##
	text	' 0.00'

Xbase GET Clause

In Xbase, interaction with the user occurs with the @ GET command. The GET command has some additional clauses that we should be able to emulate in Windows.

Emulating the VALID Clause

In Xbase, any @ Get command can have a VALID clause, which prevents the user from leaving the Get until a condition is met. We could accomplish the same thing by attaching code to the onExit /LostFocus event for the control, however, I'd like to talk you out of it. Windows users are used to having the freedom to move about the form, filling in any of the controls, in any order. By all means, display an error message if the value in the control is not appropriate, but don't keep the user mired in the control. Doing so will cause your program to behave differently from most other Windows applications, and the entire purpose of Windows is consistency for the user.

What you should do is to check all conditions when the user clicks on a button to save the form. If a certain required piece of information is missing, then display a message and stay within the form. The user can either correct the problem or abort the form.

Emulating the WHEN Clause

You can easily emulate the WHEN clause using the onEnter / GotFocus event, however, this is probably not the best way to handle such situations. You should flag all controls that are dependent upon another control as disabled. When the other control is changed, you can then enable the controls as needed. This is more in keeping with freedom of movement amongst controls, rather than the sequential processing we've gotten used to in DOS programming.

Checkbox

The checkbox control is useful when you need to get a logical value from the user. The user may select the option by using the mouse and clicking on it, or by moving to the control and pressing the space bar.

Checkbox Properties

In addition to the standard control properties, the Checkbox control has an additional property that controls how the user can interact with it. There are also two properties to let you query the state of the Checkbox at run-time.

AllowGrayed (Delphi only)

The *AllowGrayed* property determines if a check box can have two or three possible states. If AllowGrayed is False, which is the default value, clicking a Checkbox alternately checks and unchecks it. If AllowGrayed is True, clicking a check box either checks, grays, or unchecks it.

Checked /Value

The *Checked* property (in Delphi) or the *Value*=1 (checked) expression in Visual Basic is a boolean value that is only available at run-time and determines whether an option is selected. True means the control is checked and False indicates that it is not checked (or greyed, if that is permissible)

State /Value

The *State* property (in Delphi) or the*Value* property (in Visual Basic), which is only available at run-time, determines the various states a Checkbox control can have. These are the possible values:

State	Value	Meaning
cbUnchecked	0=Unchecked	Not checked, option not selected
cbChecked	1=Checked	Checked, option has been selected
cbGrayed	2=Grayed	A third state, possibly undecided

Using the Checkbox Control

Frequently, a Checkbox control will toggle the enabled flag on other controls. For example, the code fragment in Listing 4.4 shows the Edit Box for taxes being enabled or disabled depending upon what the user checks to the taxable property.

Listing 4.4 Checkbox controlling other controls.

```
procedure TSerInvoice.TaxableClick(Sender: TObject);
begin
    { Set the enabled property of the salestax edit control to whatever
the current status of the taxable checkbox control is }

    salestax.enabled := taxable.checked;
end;
```

Option/Radio Buttons

The option button or radio button controls are useful when the user should select one choice from a small list of alternatives. The user may select the option by using the mouse and clicking on it, or by moving to the control and pressing the **Spacebar**. Once the user select one option, the other options in the group are automatically deselected.

Radiobutton Properties

Radiobuttons function in a manner very similar to Checkboxes. However, there is no ability to gray out an option, so only the *Checked* property (in Delphi) or *Value* property (in Visual Basic) are applicable when using radio buttons.

Checked/Value

The *Checked* property (in Delphi) or the *Value*=1 (checked) expression is Visual Basic is a boolean value that is only available at run-time and determines whether an option is selected. True means the control is checked, and False indicates that it is not checked.

List Boxes

The *Listbox* control is a standard CUA list box. Listbox displays a list from which users can select one or more items. This is similar to the ACHOICE() function from Clipper or the @ GET FROM <array> clause in FoxPro. The Listbox control has a variety of properties for manipulating it, as well as a table of items for the user to select from.

Columns

The *Columns* property denotes the number of columns in the list box. List boxes are generally only 1 column, although you can increase the number of columns if vertical space is tight on the form and horizontal space is available.

ItemIndex /Index

The *ItemIndex* (Delphi) / *Index* (Visual Basic) property is a run-time integer that indicates the currently selected item, if any, in the list box of choices. This allows you to determine the current item's value.

Items/List

The *Items* (Delphi) / *List* (Visual Basic) property contains the strings that make up the list of items for your user to pick from. In Delphi, the Items property is a special object called tStrings. This object allows you to easily manipulate the list with the following methods and properties.

Count property number of items currently in the list
Add method adds a new string to the list
Clear method removes all entries from the list
Delete method removes a single entry from the list
LoadFromFile loads the list from a text file

In Visual Basic, the List property is an array of string values that make up the pick list. You can manipulate the array using various Visual Basic commands. You need to pass an index number to specify any individual array element or you can use FOR/NEXT loops to process the entire array.

MultiSelect Property

The *MultiSelect* property (boolean in Delphi, numeric in Visual Basic) determines whether the user can select more than one item at a time from the list. If MultiSelect is True (Delphi) or 1-Simple (Visual Basic), then the user can select multiple items. If MultiSelect if False or 0-None (which is the default), then the user can only select on item from the list. Visual Basic has a third option, 2-Extended, which allows the user to mark a group of items using the **shift** and **arrow** keys or mouse.

Sorted Property

The *Sorted* property indicates whether the items in a list box or combo box are arranged alphabetically. To sort the items, set the Sorted value to True. If Sorted is False (which is the default), the items will be unsorted. If you add or insert items when Sorted is True, they will automatically be placed in alphabetical order.

Decorative Touches

In Xbase, the @ BOX command and @ TO command are used to draw boxes and frames around various parts of the screen. Naturally, there are similar controls in

Windows. However, it is important to understand the difference between drawing lines and placing panels or frames on the form. A frame or panel is a control that Windows has to manage (and hence use resources) while lines, shapes, and bevels are more decorative components which can be placed on the form without using resources.

What are Resources Anyway?

When working with DOS, memory was one of our largest constraints. Windows' memory management is quite different from DOS, and for the most part memory issues are not as much of a problem with Windows. However, there is a different area you need to watch. The Windows operating system needs to keep track of all controls and forms and allocates some memory (called resources) to communicate with every control. As the number of forms and controls increase, resource utilization will grow. You are much more likely to run out of resources than memory in Windows.

Panels/Frames

Panels (Delphi) and *Frames* (Visual Basic) are container components that Windows must communicate with. Controls placed on top of the panel or frame are considered owned by the Panel or Frame. If the Panel or Frame is moved, then all controls placed on it must also move. This requires that Windows manages the component, which of course, takes up resources. Although for simple programs, the user of Panels and Frames probably won't make that much of a difference, you should write code to use as few resources as possible.

Bevels/Shapes

Bevels (Delphi) and *Shapes* (Visual Basic and Delphi) are components that draw on the forms, but are not container components. Windows does not need to manage these shapes, hence no resources need to be assigned. If you simply want to add decorative touches to the form by drawing boxes around sections of the form, use the Bevel or Shape and save on resources.

Many More Controls

We have only scratched the surface of the myriad of controls available for forms. Delphi alone has about 75 unique controls. Visual Basic comes with a good standard set and a large number of third-party controls are available. Take the time to explore the control boxes, their properties and methods. Any user interface you can accomplish in Xbase programming can probably be accomplished with some reasonable combination of the controls in Windows programming.

Communicating between Controls

All of the controls we place on a form are considered to be owned by the form. This allows the controls on a form to interact with one another. For example, you might want to change the phone number's editmask if the user is from outside the United States or disable the sales tax edit box if the customer is marked as tax exempt.

When you are writing event handling code, you can generally access the properties and methods of any other control on the form. This allows certain controls to impact other controls. However, keep in mind that the user is not required to go through the controls in the sequence you've designed them. Any controls that are dependent upon a particular value in another control should be disabled until that value is entered in the dependent control. You could do this buy checking the control's value in the onExit event and enabling or disabling the other controls as appropriate.

Creating a Few Forms

Let's take the time to create a few of the forms for handling our accounting application. If you refer back to Table 3.1, you will see the list of objects that our system must interact with.

Ledger and Accounts

The *Ledger* is a container object that holds the account information for the various accounts in the system. The *Account* consists of an identifying number, a short description, and a current balance. The balance should not be editable, it should be updated via journal entries.

To make our system more powerful, let's also handle budget information. The budget consists of four quarterly amounts allocated to the account. We want our system to be able to enter one budget amount and evenly divide it among the quarters or to enter the four quarterly budget amounts.

Visually Designing the Form

The first step in creating a form is to visually design the layout. You should come up with a title for the form and get a rough idea of the form's size. For the chart of accounts we need the account number, the description, the balance, and a monthly budget breakdown. Figure 4.11 shows our first draft of the form for the accounts.

Figure 4.11 Account editing form.

The account number prompt is followed by a combination box so the user can either enter an account number or look up a new one. The dollar amounts are all done using the maskedit control. And, of course, the final touch is the push buttons to allow the user to easily indicate what he or she wants to do.

The Visual Basic code in Listing 4.5 shows some of the special handling we want to do on the form. When the user enters an amount in the Y-T-D budget box, we want to take this amount and allocate it over the four quarters. We attached this code to the lostfocus event, so the amount will be updated only after we leave the control.

Listing 4.5 Visual Basic code to allocate budget amount.

```
Private Sub YTD_Amt_LostFocus()
  Private nAmt
     nAmt         = Val(YTD_Amt.Text)
     Jan_Mar.Text = Str(nAmt / 4)
     Apr_Jun.Text = Str(nAmt / 4)
     Jul_Sep.Text = Str(nAmt / 4)
     Oct_Dec.Text = Str(nAmt / 4)
End Sub
```

Checkbook

The checkbook form should mimic the checkbook that most users are familiar. Figure 4.12 shows a simple browsing screen with a few buttons attached to it. The user can click on the Write Checks or Record Deposits button, which will bring up additional forms to collect information.

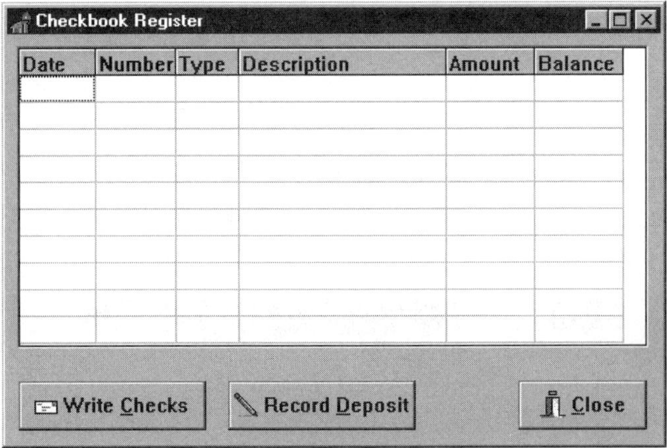

Figure 4.12 Check register screen.

Customers

The customer file would normally be stored in a DBF or similar file. In Chapter 6 we will talk about how to have our form use the data from the DBF file to populate the customer form shown in Figure 4.13.

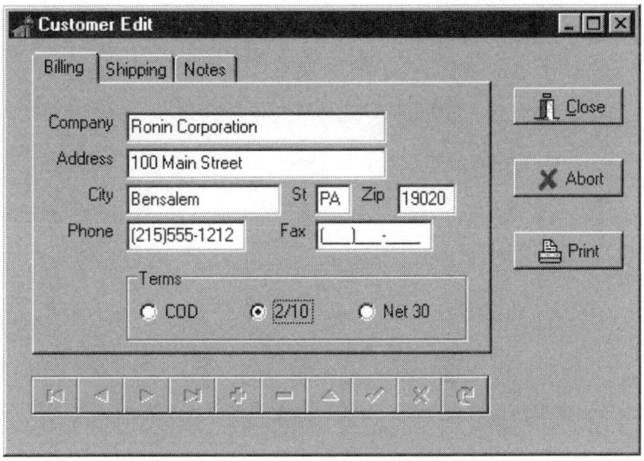

Figure 4.13 Customer edit screen.

We've chosen a tabbed notebook style to represent the customer file, with separate tabs for billing information, shipping locations, and general customer notes. The bar with arrows across the bottom of the form is a navigator bar that allows us to move through the database of customers.

Invoices

Our invoice program consists of a single form with prompts for the customer, date, and invoice number. The user can then specify the service work that was performed as well as the amount and sales tax, if any. This form was written in Delphi. Figure 4.14 illustrates the form.

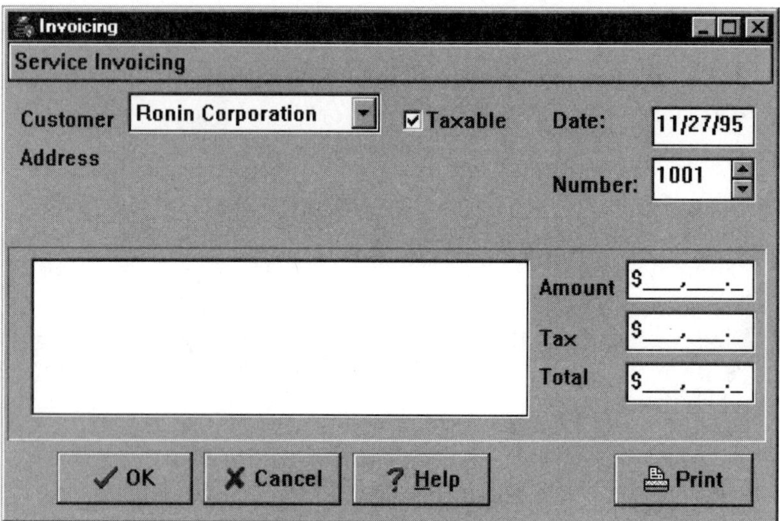

Figure 4.14 Invoice form.

Listing 4.6 shows some of the Delphi procedures attached to the form's controls. Although we would probably call a form-based report to print the invoice (which we cover in Chapter 7), the *PrintButtonClick* procedure shows one easy way to print an invoice.

Listing 4.6 Procedures attached to invoice form.

```
procedure TSerInvoice.FormCreate(Sender: TObject);
begin
   ServicesMemo.Text := '' ;  { Default the text to an empty string }
end;

procedure TSerInvoice.CancelButtonClick(Sender: TObject);
begin
   SerInvoice.close;  {close the form if cancel is clicked}
end;

procedure TSerInvoice.TaxableClick(Sender: TObject);
begin
     if not taxable.checked then       { if not taxable, then}
        salestax.enabled := false ;    { disabled the salestax edit box }
end;

procedure TSerInvoice.PrintButtonClick(Sender: TObject);
begin
     OkButton.Visible     := false;  { Turn off the buttons temporarily
}
     CancelButton.Visible := false;
     HelpButton.Visible   := false;
     PrintButton.Visible  := false;

     SerInvoice.Print;               { Print the form }

     OkButton.Visible     := true;
     CancelButton.Visible := true;   { Turn the buttons back on }
     HelpButton.Visible   := true;
     PrintButton.Visible  := true;
end;
```

Summary

We've covered a lot in this chapter. Forms and controls make up a large portion of Windows programming. In addition, the code written in Visual Basic or Delphi is in small chunks rather than monolithic, do-it-all as DOS programs tend to be. Coming from a DOS background, this can be a little disconcerting at first. However, once you've gotten used to it, you'll probably appreciate that Windows is managing a lot of the interaction with the user and freeing you to focus on the business needs of the application.

A key facet that you should keep in mind is to design and write smaller chunks of code and determine when to have the system perform this code. In DOS, we tend to develop at the top and plug in the small chunks as we go. In Windows programming, the process is reversed. We develop the small chunks of code and then decide where to put the code and how to make it available to the user. We will discuss this process more in Chapter 10.

CHAPTER 5:

WORKING WITH MENUS

In Chapter 4, the form and how to place controls on the form were discussed. In this chapter, the menu item controls and how to attach forms and actions to menu items are discussed. This chapter also covers how to alter some of the menu's properties both at design time and run-time. Finally, this chapter covers the standard and pop-up menus found in most CUA applications.

Designing Menus

Menu items in Visual Basic and Delphi are standard objects (or controls) that are used to present CUA-type menus to the user. The property inspector can be used to manipulate the controls, much like other controls; however, it is much easier to use the menu designer to create the objects.

Delphi's Menu Editor

Access Delphi's menu editor by dropping a main menu component on the form (or click on an existing one). Figure 5.1 illustrates the Delphi menu editor, which shows a visual image of the menu in a WYSIWYG (What You See Is What You Get) manner. The menu editor simplifies putting together a menu structure in Delphi.

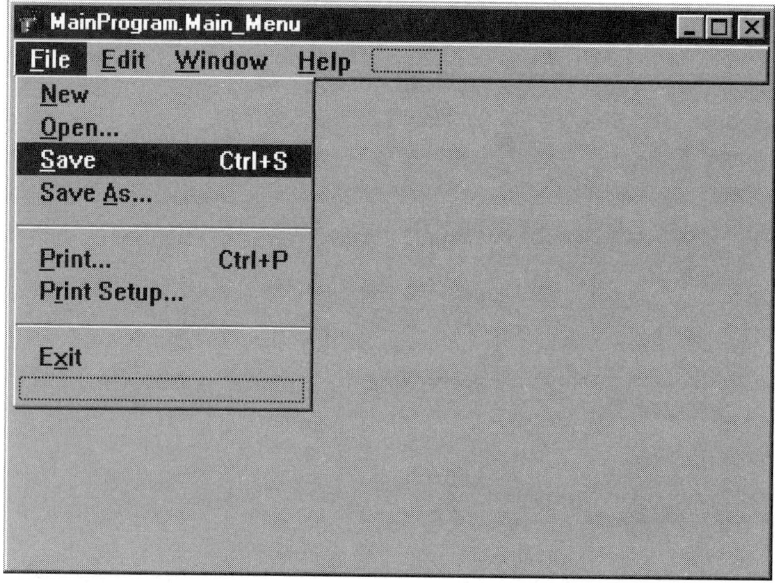

Figure 5.1 Delphi menu editor.

The Delphi menu inspector can be navigated much like the actual menu. A new menu item can be inserted by simply typing text in one of the item slots on the menu. Delphi automatically assigns a default name to the new menu. The text that is entered is assigned to the **Caption** property.

Similarly, an existing menu's caption property can be changed by editing it directly in the menu editor. The menu item's properties, can be accessed by clicking on the object inspector. Any of the properties and events for the currently selected menu item can be edited.

If a single hyphen is used for the caption, Delphi will treat the menu item as a separator bar and will draw a line across the menu box. This is handy for logically breaking a menu into sections.

Figure 5.2 shows the property inspector for the selected menu item. Although the menu items are controls like the other controls discussed in Chapter 4, the menu designer is much easier to use than manually coding menu item controls on the form.

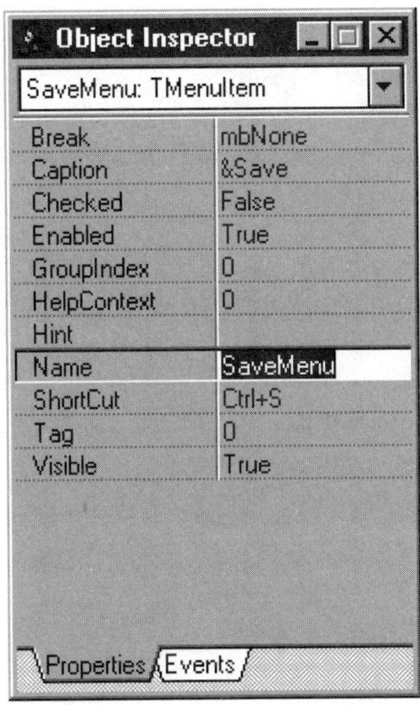

Figure 5.2 Property inspector for MenuItem object.

Nested Menus in Delphi

To add a nested menu in the Delphi menu editor, click the right mouse button while the appropriate menu item is highlighted. Figure 5.3 shows the pop-up menu that appears which allows a nested menu to be attached. Direct access to a sub-menu can be accomplished by pressing the **Ctrl-Right** key combination while on the selected item.

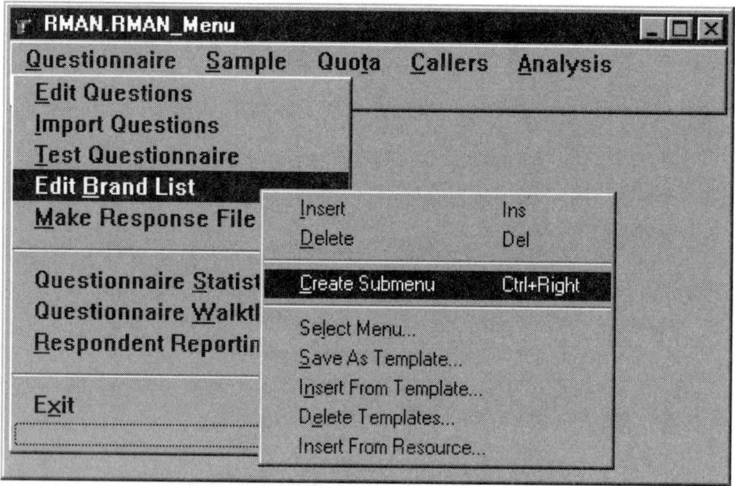

Figure 5.3 Pop-up menu in menu editor.

Submenus can be nested as deep as needed, but after one or two levels, the submenus often get confusing for the user to navigate. Besides **Insert** and **Delete**, the following options can be used to make menu design easier.

Save as Template

This option saves the current menu structure for reuse. This option is useful if a very similar menu design exists for the applications, because the existing structure can be copied directly into the menu editor to make whatever changes that are required.

Insert from Template

This option brings up any existing templates and allows them to be inserted into the menu editor. In addition to the menu templates the user might have saved, Delphi includes menu templates for the standard CUA menus, including **File**, **Edit**, **Windows**, and **Help**. The user merely needs to navigate to the desired position and insert the template. This option allows standard menus to be put together very quickly.

Visual Basic's Menu Editor

Figure 5.4 shows the menu editor in Visual Basic, which is accessed by selecting it from the main Visual Basic menu, or by using the short cut key (**Ctrl-M** in Visual Basic 3.0, and **Ctrl-E** in Visual Basic 4.0).

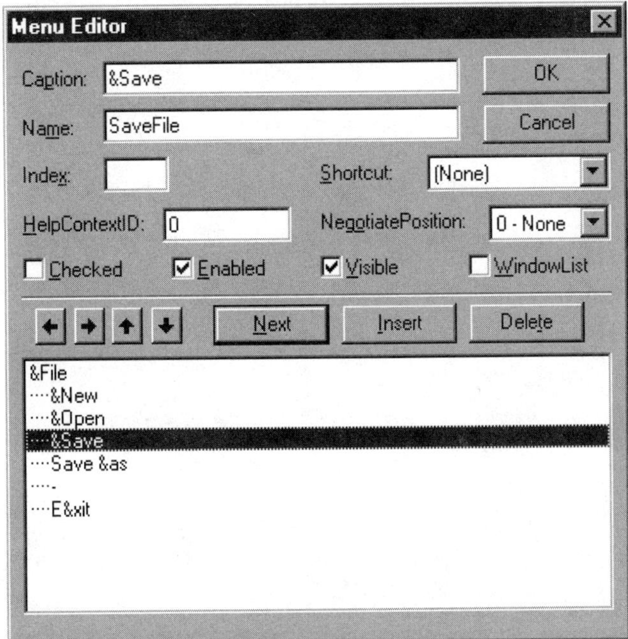

Figure 5.4 Visual Basic menu editor.

Navigation in the Visual Basic editor is different than Delphi's in that the menu is visually represented in an outline form and all the properties are accessible from the one window.

The menu editor can be navigated by moving through the outline list with either the mouse or the arrow keys. Once positioned on the desired item, the user can edit its properties in the form above the list. The most important properties are the **Caption**, which is the text that appears on the menu, and the **Name**, which allows the code to refer to the menu item. Remember to assign a name to each menu item as Visual Basic, unlike Delphi, does not automatically assign names.

A separator bar is created in Visual Basic at the indicated position by putting a single hyphen character as the menu item's caption. The separator bar should be given a name even though it is very unlikely its properties will be adjusted at run time.

Nested Menus in Visual Basic

Nested menus in Visual Basic are created by clicking on the **right arrow** button in the menu editor. The currently highlighted menu item will be indented one level each time you click the **right arrow**. Clicking the **level arrow** will bring it back one level. Figure 5.5 shows a nested menu structure in the menu editor.

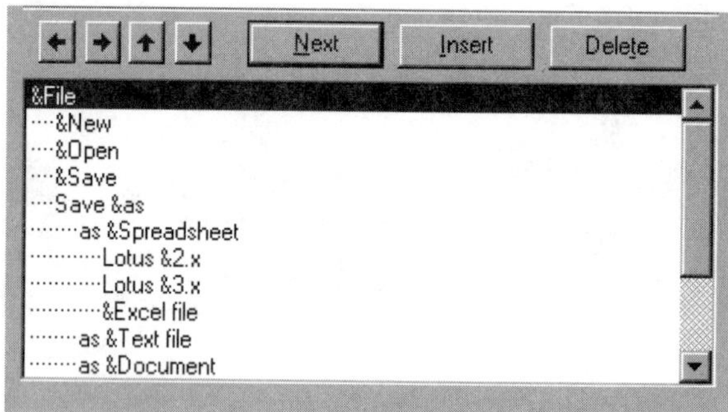

Figure 5.5 Nested structure in menu editor.

The result of this nested structure is shown in Figure 5.6.

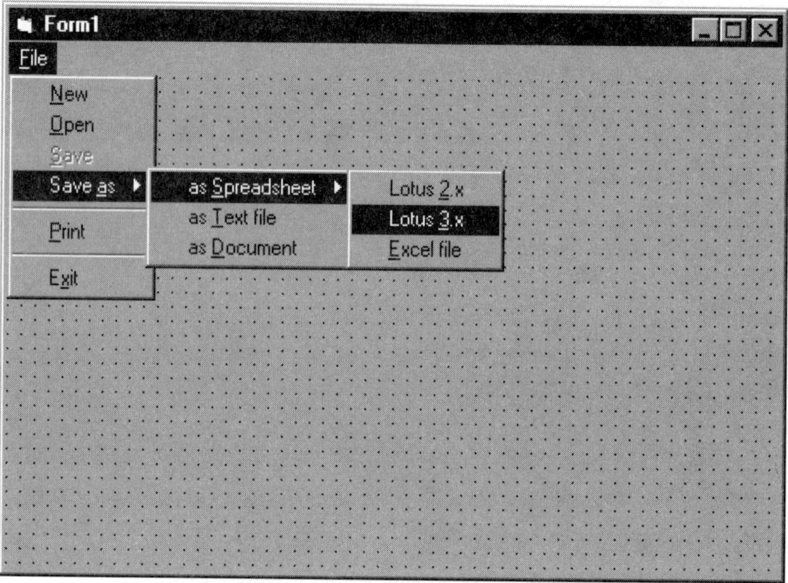

Figure 5.6 Nested menu from Visual Basic.

Control Arrays for Menu Items

In addition to nested menus, Visual Basic also provides a method of storing menu objects in an array. The benefit of this approach is that one function can be written to perform the click action, relying upon an index to the array element that Visual Basic will automatically pass as a parameter. For example, the code in Listing 5.1 creates an event handler to handle interaction with the Windows clipboard:

Listing 5.1 Clipboard code via event handler.

```
Private sub menuEdit_Click( Index as Integer)
select case Index
case 0              ' User clicked on Cut
 Clipboard.clear
 Clipboard.setText TextEditBox.SelText
 TextEditBox.SelText = ""
case 1              ' User clicked on Copy
 Clipboard.clear
 Clipboard.setText TextEditBox.SelText
case 2              ' User clicked on Paste
 TextEditBox.SelText = Clipboard.GetText()
end select
End Sub
```

In this code fragment, Visual Basic looks at the index property from the currently selected menu item and uses that property as an array index and passes it to the menuEdit_Click function.

To set up a control array in the menu editor, enter the same name for the menu items, but vary their **index** property. Visual Basic requires each menu item in the control array to be indented to the same level. In addition, the items must appear contiguously in the menu outline.

Menu Properties

The menu designers allow interactive creation of MenuItem controls. Just like the other controls, the MenuItem controls have properties and events associated with them.

Appearance (Visual Basic)

The **Appearance** property, only available in Visual Basic. determines whether the menu item should have a three-dimensional appearance. If Appearance contains **1-3D,** then three-dimensional effects will be used, whereas **0-Flat** indicates three-dimensional effects will not be used.

Break (Delphi)

The **Break** property, only available in Delphi, breaks a long menu into two or more columns. The possible values for the property are as follows:

Value	Meaning
mbNone	No menu breaking occurs, this is the default.
mbBarBreak	The menu breaks into another column with the selected menu item appearing at the top of the new column. A bar separates the new and the old columns.
mbBreak	The menu breaks into another column with the menu item appearing at the top of the new column. Only space separates the new and the old columns.

Caption

The **Caption** property is a string value that contains the text contents of the label. To underline a character in a string, include an ampersand (&) before the character. This type of character, called an *accelerator* character, allows the user to select the menu item by pressing **Alt** and the underlined character.

For menu items, the **Caption** property can be used to create a line that separates the menu into parts, by specifying a hyphen (-) as the value of **Caption.**

Checked

The **Checked** property determines whether or not a checkmark character should appear to the left of the menu choice. Checked is a logical value, with True causing the check to appear and False, the default, resulting in no check mark.

This property is typically set to its desired state at design time and then changed, if needed, at run time. If for example, the menu choice is a toggle, the check character may be used to indicate the current state of the option. The check indicates that the option was selected and absence of the check indicates that the option was not selected.

Enabled

The **Enabled** property is a logical value that controls whether the menu item can be selected by the user. If **Enabled** is True, the user can select the menu items with either the mouse or the keyboard. If **Enabled** is False, the menu ignores mouse clicks and key-presses. In addition, a disabled menu choice will appear dimmed.

Hint (Delphi)

The **Hint** property, only available in Delphi, specifies a string that will appear whenever the user moves the mouse over the menu item. This allows the user to see what the menu option will do without them actually clicking on the menu. **Hint** is available with most of the controls in Delphi.

Index / ComponentIndex

The **Index** property (Visual Basic) / **ComponentIndex** property (Delphi) is a read-only numeric property that indicates the currently selected menu item at run time.

Name

The **Name** property contains the name of the component as referenced by other components. By default, Delphi assigns sequential names based on the type of the component, such as 'MenuItem1', 'MenuItem2', and so on. These names may be changed to suit your needs. Visual Basic does not automatically assign names, but requires every menu option be given a name. These names will be used at run time to specify the menu item in which you wish to work.

ShortCut

The **ShortCut** property determines which key stroke key stroke, if any, that can be used to access a menu item. The key combination that can be used appears to the right of the menu item in the menu.

Usually **ShortCut** is set for menu items in the Object Inspector (Delphi) or the Menu Editor (Visual Basic), which give a long list of options to choose from. If menu items are created at run time, however, you can still create shortcuts for them.

Tag

The **Tag** property is a user-defined slot that is available to store an integer value (in Delphi) or a string value (in Visual Basic) as part of a component. Nothing is done with the **Tag** property, it is merely carried around with the object; it is up to your code to make use of the property, if needed. For CA-Clipper users, this property is similar to the **Cargo** instance variable from the various objects.

Visible

The **Visible** property is a logical value that determines whether or not the user can see the menu item. In order for the user to interact with the menu, **Visible** must be True. However, even if **Visible** is False, your program can still work with the menu item's properties.

Standard Menus

Most Windows applications following the CUA recommendations and use some standard menus for certain type of operations. These menus—**File**, **Edit**, **Window**, and **Help**—should be used whenever feasible within an application.

When the menus are used, place the **File** menu first, followed by the **Edit** menu. Menus unique to the application should follow with the final menu items being the **Window** and the **Help** menus.

File Menu

If application opens any kind of files, such as memos, E-Mail, databases, etc. then you should include a File Menu which allows the user to create new files, open existing ones, and save their work to a file. Figure 5.7 shows the standard file menu generated in a Delphi application.

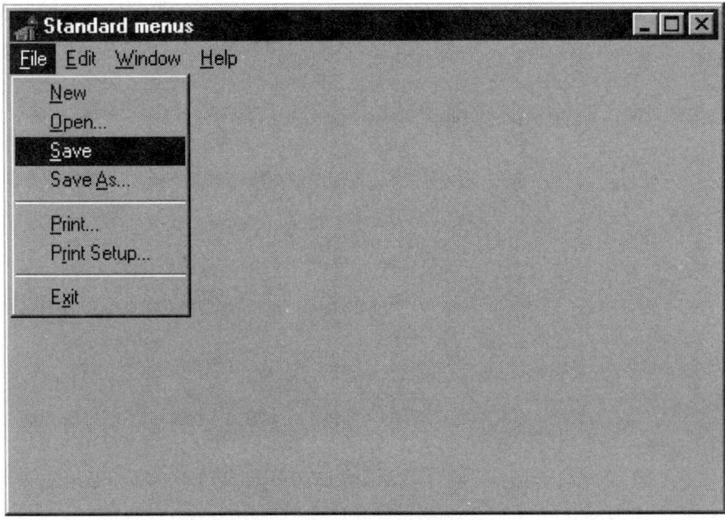

Figure 5.7 Standard file menu.

Creating a file menu is rather simple and the standard menus (**File**, **Edit**, **Window**, and **Help**) are accessible in the Delphi templates while designing menus in Delphi.

New Option

The **New** menu option creates a new file or document in memory, usually with a default name. If the application can create multiple types of files, a submenu of choices should be presented as to which kind of file to work with. Once the user selected a file type, the created window should reflect the file type in its default naming convention.

In MDI applications, where multiple documents might be opened simultaneously, attach a numeric label indicating the occurrence of the file. If programming an SDI application and the new option causes closing of an existing file, be sure to ask the user if they want to save changes before opening the new file.

Open Option

The **Open** menu option presents a dialog box that allows the user to select a file either in the current directory or allows them to navigate to another directory. Fortunately, Windows has a standard file opening dialog box, so much of the work is already done. We will discuss standard Windows dialog boxes in Chapter 7.

Once the file is selected, it is loaded into the application's memory, which allows the user to manipulate it.

Save Option

The **Save** menu option should save the current file to the disk. If the file name is already known, then the save command should write the contents to that file without presenting any dialog to the user. If no file name has been specified, the Save As dialog box should be called allowing the user to specify the file name.

Save As Option

The **Save As** menu option allows the user to save the current document under a different file name. Windows has a standard dialog to allow the user to specify the file name and directory. Once the user specifies a file name, the application should write the document to the indicated file name.

Print Option

The **Print** menu option prints the current document on the currently selected printer. The user may control the print job by specifying a page range, number of copies, and so on.

Print Setup Option

The **Print Setup** menu option should display a dialog box that allows the user to select any printer and optionally configure the select printer. Fortunately, the Print Setup dialog box is a standard one in Windows, so it will only require minimal coding. (We will cover this in more detail in Chapter 7.)

Exit Option

The **Exit** menu option allows the user to gracefully (i.e. not via a GPF) finish using the program. **Exit** is most often found as the last choice on the file menu. If a file menu does not exist, place **Exit** as the bottom choice of the left-most menu. It's always a good idea to give the user the option to save his current work before exiting.

Edit Menu

The Edit menu, which should immediately follow the File menu if one exists, allows the user to perform standard editing operations, such as undo, cut, copy, and paste. Figure 5.8 shows a standard Edit menu.

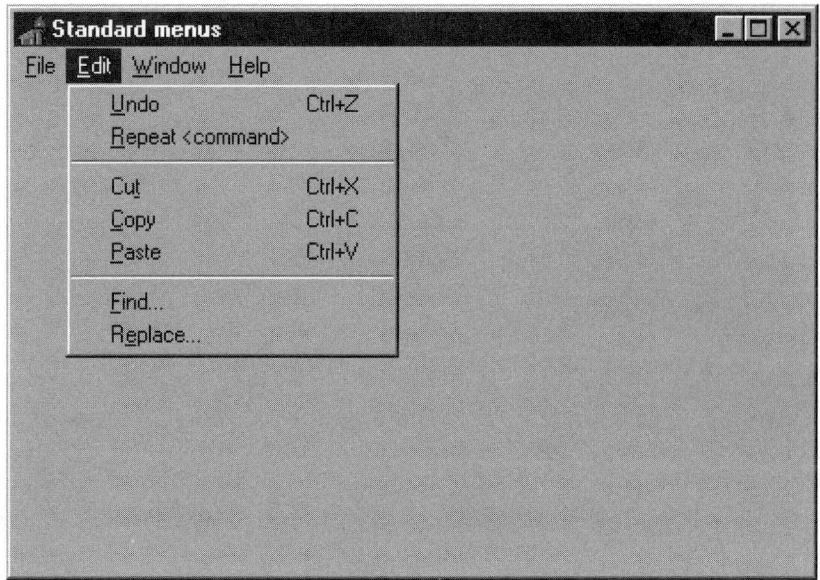

Figure 5.8 Standard Edit menu.

Undo Option

The **Undo** menu option allows the user to reverse the last command. **Undo** usually has a shortcut key of **Ctrl-Z**. Many programs provide multiple levels of undo ability, where the user can continually move backwards until they restore almost any changes made. A good undo capability gives the user a great deal of confidence to experiment and makes them feel more comfortable with your software.

Although it takes a bit of work to design a good undo capability, it will be time well spent and appreciated by the user. However, if some operations cannot be undone, be sure to warn the user that the process cannot be reversed. It would be unfortunate if a user became comfortable with the undo process, and subsequently discovered that a major error they just made cannot be undone.

Repeat Option

The **Repeat** menu option repeats the last action and usually indicates the name of the action to be repeated in the menu's caption (i.e., repeat paste or repeat copy). **Repeat** is a time-saver that, if it is included, should follow **Undo** on the Edit menu. However, be careful about how **Repeat** is used. Imagine a scenario where the user increased prices in a spreadsheet file by 5%. A second repeat command will increased prices by another 5%, for a cumulative total of 10.25%, not 10% as some users might suspect.

Cut Option

The **Cut** menu option takes the currently selected text and copies it to the Clipboard (a special temporary storage area Windows provides for applications to share data). Once the data is copied to the Clipboard, it is cleared out. The **Cut** option usually has a shortcut key of **Ctrl-X.**

Copy Option

The **Copy** menu option takes the currently selected text and copies it to the Clipboard, just as the **Cut** option does. However, the data is not cleared out after it is copied. The **Copy** option usually has a shortcut key of **Ctrl-C.**

Paste Option

The **Paste** menu options take the current contents of the Clipboard and copies it to the currently selected text area where the cursor awaits input. The Clipboard's contents are not erased.

Find Option

If appropriate for your application, a Find dialog box should be provided to allow the user to search for particular text. Windows provides a standard Find dialog box, which can be used to simplify getting the information from the user. The information is then searched for and the display repositioned to show the found information. If nothing is found, an error message should be displayed to the user.

Replace Option

The **Replace** menu option works similarly to the **Find** option, except that the found text can be replaced with a new value. If appropriate for your application, you should provide a Replace dialog box as well as a Find dialog box. Windows provides a standard Replace dialog box, which can be used to simplify user interaction. Then, search for the information and replace the found text. If the user has requested, pause and allow confirmation before the text is replaced. If nothing is found, an error message should be displayed.

Window Menu

If the application allows the opening of multiple files or views of the same file, then you should provide a Window menu that allows the user to manipulate the windows opened by the program. Figure 5.9 illustrates a standard Window menu.

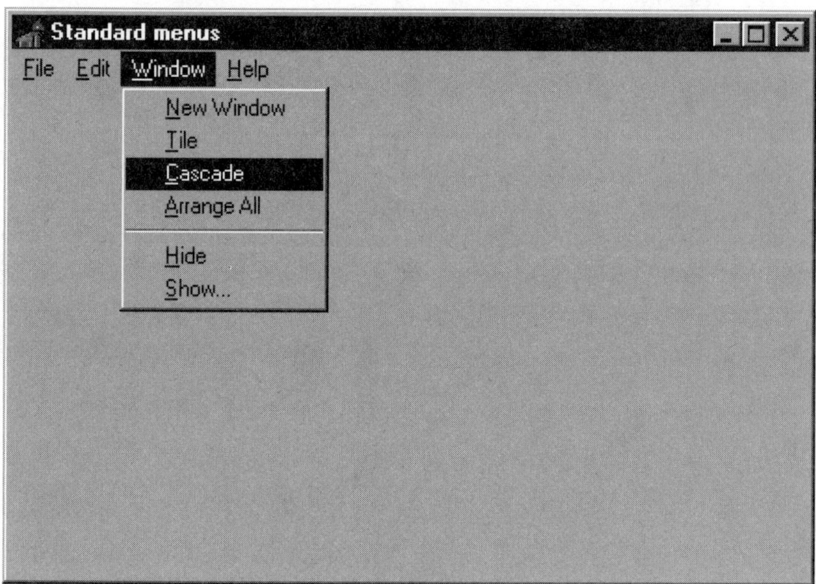

Figure 5.9 Standard Window menu.

New Window Option

The **New Window** menu option creates another view of the current document in a separate window. It is not the same as the **File/New** option, which loads a new document into a window. Once the window is added, its name should be appended to the window menu, allowing the user to easily navigate through multiple windows. For example, Figure 5.10 shows the Window menu from Ami Pro with a few of this book's chapters opened.

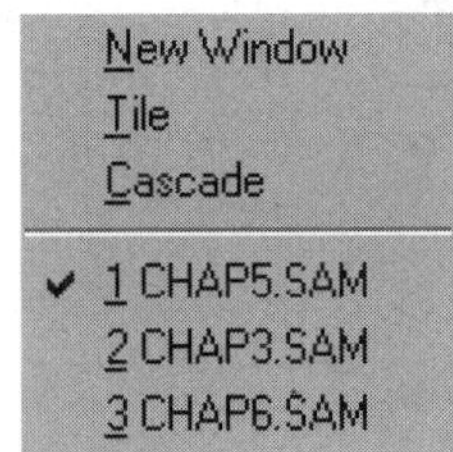

Figure 5.10 Window menu with multiple open windows.

The user can easily switch between windows by selecting the named window from the list of choices below the separator bar. Note the use of the checked property to indicate the current document.

Tile Option

The **Tile** menu option arranges the windows in the workspace in a manner that shows each window without overlapping. Fortunately, for MDI applications, the **Tile** command is built into the Windows programming languages, so programmers don't have to determine how to tile the windows, merely request Windows to do it (via the **Tile** method in Delphi and the **Arrange(vbTileHorizontal)** or **Arrange(vbTileVertical)** function calls in Visual Basic). Figure 5.11 shows a number of windows from AmiPro after a tile operation.

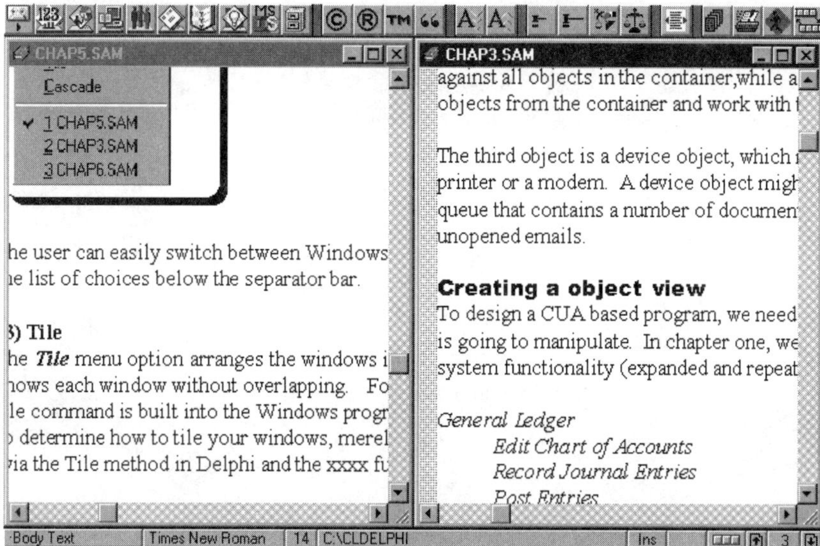

Figure 5.11 Tiled windows.

Cascade Option

The **Cascade** menu option arranges the windows in the workspace in a manner that shows each window overlapping, much like a stack of cards. Again, for MDI applications, the **Cascade** command is built into the programming languages, so programmers don't have to determine how to cascade the windows, merely have Windows do it (via the **Cascade** method in Delphi and the **Arrange(vbCascade)** function call in Visual Basic).

Figure 5.12 shows a number of windows from AmiPro after a cascade operation is performed.

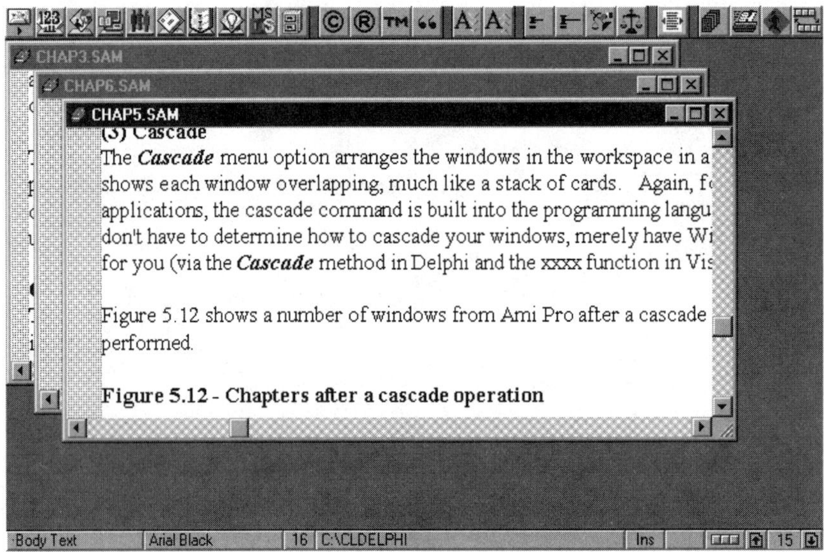

Figure 5.12 Chapters after a cascade operation.

Arrange All Option

The **Arrange All** menu option is used to handle other arrangements of windows, depending upon what would be most appropriate for the application. An **Arrange Icons** menu option might be provided to control the display of minimized windows within your program. Visual Basic has a **vbArrangeIcons** parameter that can be passed to the arrange function call and Delphi has an **ArrangeIcons** method on its form objects.

Hide Option

The **Hide** menu option should set the **Visible** property of the current window to False so it cannot be seen by the user. The window can still be manipulated, but until the user shows the hidden window (possibly by selecting it from the window list), he or she cannot interact with it.

Show Option

The **Show** menu option sets the **Visible** property of the current window to True and allows the user to interact with it.

Help Menu

On-line help is standard in most Windows applications and it should probably be included in your applications. If a Help menu is included, it should always be the right-most menu on the menu bar. Figure 5.13 shows the standard Help menu options.

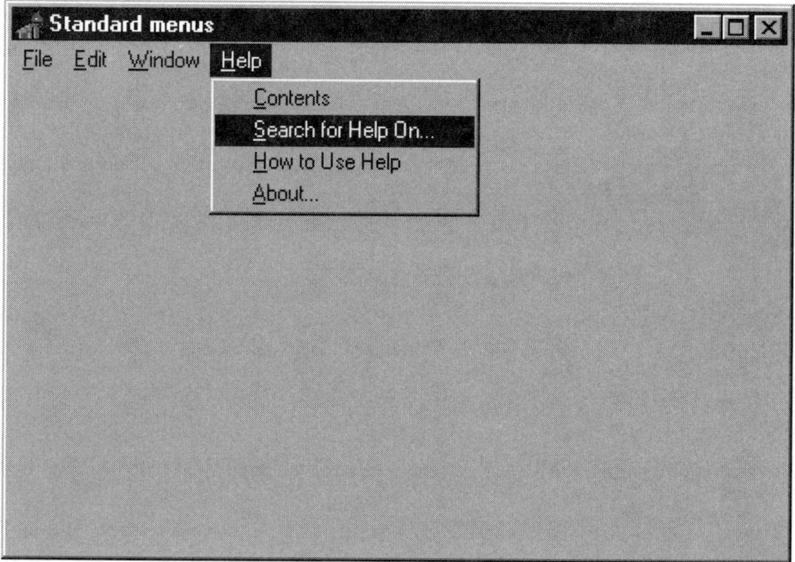

Figure 5.13 Standard help menu.

Contents Option

The **Contents** menu option displays an ordered listing of the various topics available in the on-line help guide. This is typically done via the **WinHelp** function with the **Contents** parameter (see **Writing Help Files** on the next page).

Search for Help On Option

The **Search for Help On** menu option allows the user to type in a string of text and attempt to find matching help material. This is done via a keyword list maintained in the **Help** file. Each keyword has a list of attached topics the user can access once the appropriate keyword is found.

How to Use Help Option

The **How to Use Help** menu option would typically display a window that provides instructions to the user about how to use the help system. This also is handled by the **WinHelp()** API function call.

About Option

The **About** menu option should display a dialog box that displays information about your application. The box should include, at a minimum, the application's name and copyright notice, as well as an **OK** button to close the window. Most programs also include a graphic of some kind and a lot of legalese with serial number. Because most users will go to this screen to learn their serial number, consider writing other information here that might be helpful during a tech-support call, such as memory usage and/or free disk space.

Writing Help Files

Designing Windows help files is an art in and of itself. The basic process involves creating a **Rich Text** file which is processed by the **Help** compiler into a **HLP** file. This **HLP** file can then be accessed via standard commands from both Delphi and Visual Basic. The details of creating Windows help, however, are beyond the scope of this book.

Once a Windows help file is created, WinHelp() can be used to access the help file. The **WinHelp()** function is part of the Windows API and expects the name of the help file and a numeric command option as parameters.

The command options can be:

HELP_CONTEXT—Looks for a particular entry in the help file

HELP_CONTENTS—Displays the table of contents

HELP_HELPONHELP—Displays help on how to use help

As the command options illustrate, it is fairly easy to insert the help file into your menu structure. Perhaps the most complex part is deciphering how the language interfaces directly to the Windows API.

Attaching Code to Menus

As we explored in Chapter 4, code can be attached to various events on forms. Fortunately, this is rather easy with menu items, because there is only one event, the **onClick** (Delphi) / **Click** (Visual Basic) event. This event is triggered whenever the user selects the menu item, either by clicking on it, by pressing **Enter** or using the menu's accelerator key.

The event code can be reached in Delphi by navigating the menu to the desired property and double-clicking or by selecting the event tab in the object inspector. In Visual Basic, navigate the menu after it has been designed and click on the desired menu choice. This will bring up the code editor for the **Click** procedure of that particular menu choice.

Closing the Form

Almost every time you write a program, you will have a **Close** menu option available. This option is usually labeled 'E&xit', with **Alt-X** as the accelerator key. The shortcut key is generally **Alt-F4**. Listing 5.2 shows sample code from Delphi to close the form. The code is attached to the **Exit** menus onClick Event handler.

Listing 5.2 Closing the form in Delphi.

```
procedure TForm1.ExitmenuClick(Sender: TObject);
begin
 close;
end;
```

Controlling the Clipboard

As with the standard edit menu, the user should be able to transfer text to and from the Windows clipboard. Listing 5.3 shows some code from Visual Basic that allows the user to manipulate the Clipboard from various menu options.

Listing 5.3 Clipboard functions in Visual Basic.

```
Private sub menuCut_Click()
 Clipboard.clear
 Clipboard.setText TextEditBox.SelText
 TextEditBox.SelText = ""
End Sub

Private sub menuCopy_Click()
```

```
 Clipboard.clear
 Clipboard.setText = TextEditBox.SelText
End Sub

Private sub menuPaste_Click()
 TextEditBox.SelText = Clipboard.GetText()
End Sub
```

Calling Forms from Menu Options

In most DOS applications, selecting an item from the menu leads to some sort of screen (or form in Delphi/VB speak). Many of the menu options will do the same thing, load and start a form. In Delphi, this is done via the **Show** method while in Visual Basic, it is the Load command that loads and displays a form.

A Small Example System

Listing 5.4 shows the Delphi code for a few menu options from the standard menu. It is provided just to show a simple example of what a Windows program in Delphi might look like.

Listing 5.4 Simple Delphi code example.

```
procedure TForm1.ExitmenuClick(Sender: TObject);
begin
 close; { close the form and exit the program }
end;

{ The next two procedures enable the save option on the menu }


procedure TForm1.Open1Click(Sender: TObject);
begin
 SaveFile.Enabled := true ;
end;

procedure TForm1.New1Click(Sender: TObject);
```

```
begin
 SaveFile.Enabled := true ;
end;

{ Call the aboutBox form and display it }

procedure TForm1.About1Click(Sender: TObject);
begin
 AboutBox.Show;
end;

procedure TForm1.Cut1Click(Sender: TObject);
begin
 Memo1.CutToClipboard;
end;

procedure TForm1.Copy1Click(Sender: TObject);
begin
 memo1.CopyToClipboard;
end;

procedure TForm1.Paste1Click(Sender: TObject);
begin
 memo1.PasteFromClipboard;
end;

procedure TForm1.SaveFileClick(Sender: TObject);
var nHandle: shortint;
 Buffer: PChar;
 Size: Byte;
begin
 Size := memo1.GetTextLen; {Get length of string in Edit1}
 Inc(Size); {Add room for null character}
 GetMem(Buffer, Size); {Creates Buffer variable}
 Memo1.GetTextBuf(Buffer,Size); {Puts MemoText into Buffer}
```

```
  nHandle := _lcreat( 'text.txt',0);
  _lwrite(nHandle,Buffer,Size);
  _Lclose(nHandle);

  FreeMem(Buffer, Size); {Frees memory from Buffer}
end;
```

The **SaveFileClick** function illustrates what Delphi code looks like. While some of the memory allocation routines may seem unusual coming from a Xbase background, most of the code is very readable and easy to comprehend. Both Delphi and Visual Basic can be used to produce very readable code.

Manipulating Menus at Run-Time

Although the menu designers provide an easy way to create menus, often times there is a need to change some of the properties at run-time. For example, if no document is opened, the **Save** menu option should be disabled. Once a document is opened, however, **Save** should be enabled by setting its enabled property to True.

Changing Menu Properties at Run-Time

The most important part of changing properties is understanding how to reference the individual menu items. Once the item is referenced its property values can be changed or its methods called. Fortunately, it is very easy to reference the menu item. Simply remember its name, which is why the menuItem1 names from Delphi probably should be changed to something more meaningful.

Imagine the standard File menu with **New**, **Open**, **Save**, and **Save As**. Assume the meaningful names of **NewMenuItem**, **OpenMenuItem**, **SaveMenuItem**, and **SaveAsMenuItem** were used. Further assume we want to have **Save** and **Save As** initially disabled and opening a new file should enable **Save As** and opening an existing file should enable both the **Save** and **Save As** options. Listing 5.5 shows some Visual Basic code that accomplishes our goals.

Listing 5.5 Visual Basic program to change run-time properties.

```
Private Sub NewMenuItem_Click()
 SaveAsMenuItem.Enabled = True
End Sub

Private Sub OpenMenuItem_Click()
 SaveMenuItem.Enabled = True
 SaveAsMenuItem.Enabled = True
End Sub

Private Sub ExitMenuItem_Click()
 unload form1
 End
End Sub
```

Adding Menu Items Dynamically at Run Time

Sometimes menu items are added to an existing menu structure while the application is running to provide more information or options to the user. There are two approaches that can solve this problem. The first is to add the menus at design time with the **Visible** property set to False and change **Visible** to True as needed. The second option is to create new items by actually adding the new menu item objects at run time.

Making Menu Items Visible

Review the **File** menu example from Listing 5.5. Assume two additional menu options, **PrintMenuItem** and **PrintSetupMenuItem**, were added at design time and the **Visible** property is set to false. We don't want these options to appear until the user opens a document. Listing 5.6 shows the modified versions of the click functions that will accomplish this.

Listing 5.6 Adding the printer menus options at run-time.

```
Private Sub NewMenuItem_Click()
 SaveAsMenuItem.Enabled = True
 PrintMenuItem.Visible = True
 PrintSetupMenuItem.Visible = True
End Sub

Private Sub OpenMenuItem_Click()
 SaveMenuItem.Enabled = True
 SaveAsMenuItem.Enabled = True
 PrintMenuItem.Visible = True
 PrintSetupMenuItem.Visible = True
End Sub
```

Adding New Menus Objects at Run Time

There are times when it is not feasible to know in advance how many additional menus might be added. In these cases, a flexible structure must be created that can have menu items added to it. Fortunately, although this takes a bit more work than setting the **Visible** property, it is still fairly easy to accomplish.

Dynamic Menus in Visual Basic

In order to create dynamic menus in Visual Basic, a control array of menu items must be created. This is done using the menu designer by specifying a menu name and an index number of zero. You might want to make the caption a separator bar and set the **Visible** property to False so that the menu will not appear until you add some additional menu options below it.

For our example, assume we have created a menu control array called MrlList with a separator bar for the caption and **Visible** set to False. Each time we click on the **New** menu option, we will add an entry to the bottom of the File menu showing the new file name.

In addition to setting up the menu control array, a variable to hold the count of menu items must be declared. Visual Basic has a section called *general* which can be used to set up module wide declaractions. In the editor window, click on the object drop-down box and select **general**. Then, click on the **proc:** drop-down box and select **declaractions.**

In this section of the code, a public variable declaration is added to hold the count of menu items.

```
Public mrl_count As Integer
```

To dynamically add to the menu, we can attach the code in Listing 5.7 to the New menu option's click handler.

Listing 5.7 Add new menus dynamically in Visual Basic.

```
Private Sub NewMenuItem_Click()

 MrlList(0).Visible = True ' Show the separator bar
 mrl_count = mrl_count + 1 ' Increment our public variable

 Load MrlList(mrl_count) ' Load new menu item and set
 MrlList(mrl_count).Caption = "test" + Str(mrl_count) ' properties
 MrlList(mrl_count).Visible = True '

End Sub
```

Each time the new menu item is clicked, the mrl_count variable is incremented and a new menu item is placed into the next element of the control array. Finally, the properties are set to allow the menu to appear under the separator bar.

Dynamic Menus in Delphi

To dynamically create new menus in Delphi, first declare the menu item as a variable of type TMenuItem. Delphi is a strongly typed language, as opposed to Xbase and Visual Basic. In Delphi, therefore, you must declare a variable type for every variable you use in your application.

The following shows such a variable declaration, where NewItem represents the **Name** property for the menu item you are adding:

```
var
 NewItem: TMenuItem;
```

Once the variable is declared, a procedure must be written which will add the newly created menu item into an existing menu. Listing 5.8 shows an example where clicking on the new menu option causes this.

Listing 5.8 Add new menu item into existing menu.

```
procedure TForm1.NewMenuClick(Sender: TObject);
begin
 NewItem := TMenuItem.Create(FileMenu);
 NewItem.Caption := 'A new menu command';
 FileMenu.AtInsert(1, NewItem);
end;
```

The first line of this procedure—not the procedure declaration itself—calls the **Create** method to create a new item in the **File** menu. The next line specifies a caption for the item. The last line calls the **Insert** method, which takes the values for where and what to insert. The first parameter, 1, specifies the second position in the menu's list, since the first position is always zero.

Pop-Up Menus

The discussion of the menu has only talked about the main menu of an application. Yet the CUA standards have another type of menu, called the *pop-up menu*. A pop-up menu is a list of menu choices in a floating box, i.e., not attached to an option in the top menu bar.

A pop-up menu's contents will vary depending upon where the mouse cursor is when the menu is invoked (using by the right mouse click). This allows you to attach pop-up menus to the form itself or to various components on the form.

Creating Pop-Up Menus

To create a pop-up menu in Delphi, simply click on the pop-up menu button and drop it somewhere on the form. The pop-up menu's position is not important since it is controlled by Windows are run-time and the image on the form is merely there for convenience of accessing it, not for positioning purposes.

Once the pop-up menu button is clicked, its contents can be edited in the same manner as the main menu, except you will not be able to create a top menu bar. The code can be attached to its event handlers and create submenus if needed, although pop-up menus generally shouldn't be nested very deeply.

Figure 5.14 shows an example of a pop-up menu attached to a memo editing control.

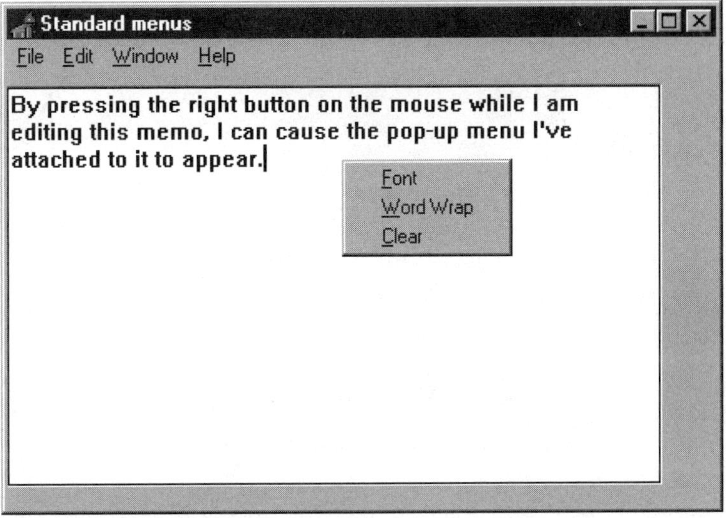

Figure 5.14 Pop-up menu for memo editing.

To create a pop-up menu (also called ***Context menu)*** in Visual Basic, create a new form and invoke the Menu Editor. Then design your menu with a top bar prompt and the choices designed underneath it. Set the top bar's **Visible** property to False to prevent it from appearing on the main menu. Figure 5.15 provides an example.

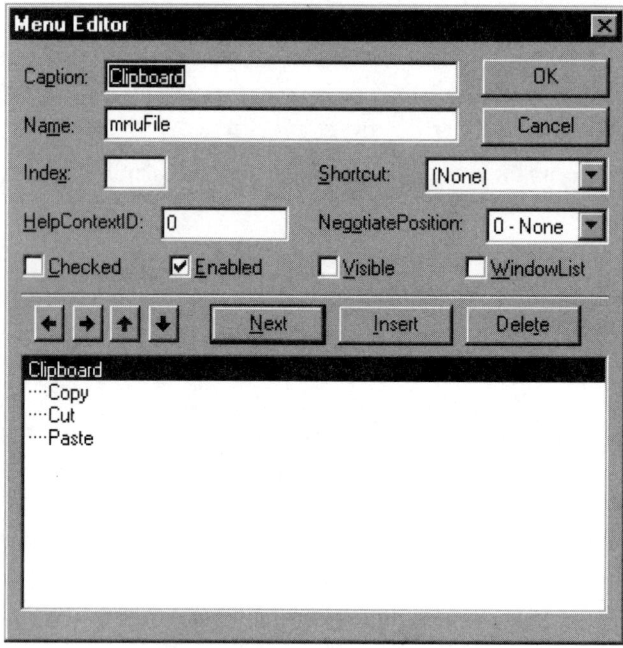

Figure 5.15 Pop-up menu in menu editor.

Once the menu has been created, add the following Visual Basic code to the form's declaration section. When a button on the mouse is pressed this routine gets called and checks for the right mouse button. If the right mouse button was pressed, the **PopupMenu** command gets called with the name of the menu to pop-up.

```
Private Sub Form_MouseDown(Button As Integer, Shift As Integer,
X As Single, Y As Single)
 If Button = 2 Then
   PopupMenu mnuFile
 End If
End Sub
```

Attaching Pop-Up Menus to the Form

One of the properties in the form object is the name of the pop-up menu that is associated with the object. To attach a pop-up menu, simply enter the menu's name in the **PopupMenu** property in the form property list. Some components also have pop-up menu properties, so you can attach different pop-up menus, complete with actions, can be attached to various components as well as the form itself.

Summary

The visual menu editing tools in both Delphi and Visual Basic make it very easy to create menus in applications. It will probably take longer to design your menu structure on paper than it will to enter it onto your form. With only one event associated with the menu item control, it is easy to attach code to execute the menu item. No matter how the user selects the menu item, Windows will execute this Click event and run the correct code.

Strive to work within the CUA guidelines, using the existing standard menus when possible, and adding your own within the proper area of the top bar. Doing this will make your program feel more comfortable to its user. Don't hesitate to use pop-up menus for those special options that need to be attached to your program. Most Windows applications use menus quite a bit and they should be in your program.

CHAPTER 6:

ACCESSING YOUR DATA

In Xbase languages, all access to DBF files is handled through a work area. In Delphi and Visual Basic, there are no work areas. In this chapter we will explore how to can work with existing DBF files without using the work area, but instead using objects to access the data.

What Exactly Is a Work Area Anyway?

When most programmers begin to work with an Xbase platform, one of the biggest areas of confusion is the concept of the work area. Other programming languages do not use the work area concept, preferring to use file handles and other arcane syntax to access databases.

Each work area is a table in memory. This table contains various status information, such as the current record number, the number of records in the file and a flag indicating end of file. In addition, a copy of all the field names and values for the current record are kept in this table. Many Xbase functions, such as **EOF()** and **RECNO()**, etc. return values from this table.

In addition to status and variables, the work area also contains commands which allow you to navigate through your database. As you move between records, a copy of the fields from the current record is always placed into the work area.

Table 6.1 shows an example of a work area table in Xbase.

Table 6.1 Example Work Area Table

Entry name	Data type	Description
BOF()	Logical	Before first record in file?
EOF()	Logical	Past last record in file?
RECNO()	Numeric	Current record number
FCOUNT()	Numeric	Number of fields
Field information	Array	
Fieldname()	Character	Current field name
Fieldtype()	Character	Field type
FieldLength()	Numeric	Length of current field

The number of work area tables varies among Xbase platforms, although 250 is the most common number. Each entry is this table serves as a communication's conduit between the actual data in the DBF file and the application's code.

Internally, this table might look like a grid, with 250 rows and a number of columns. One column contains a numeric field with the current record number; another column contains a logical field indicating EOF. Table 6.2 shows such a grid structure.

Table 6.2 Work Area Grid

#	Alias	bof()	eof()	recno()	fcount()	used()	Filter
1	Customer	.F.	.F.	14	28	.T.	
2	Invoices	.F.	.F.	384	12	.T.	cust_num='1015'
3	Vendor	.F.	.F.	62	35	.T.	
4							
5							

The Xbase language we are using will update all of the columns in the table as we move files in and out of the work area or reposition the current record. Your application can then edit the field information, and optionally write the changed information back into the associated DBF file.

CA-Clipper took advantage of this structure to create Replaceable Data Drivers (known as RDDs). Clipper allows any work area to have its own set of code for handling communications with the application. As long as the RDD works within these rules, the application code can transparently interact with the file. The file could be any type of structure that can be represented by rows and columns, such as DBF files, comma delimited ASCII files, or spreadsheets.

Xbase Work Area Equivalents

The functionality that existed with work areas in Xbase is available in both Delphi and Visual Basic, with slightly different names. The key difference is that rather than a work area table, Delphi and Visual Basic use an object to communicate between your program and the DBF file.

Delphi's TTable Object

Delphi's ***TTable*** object is the conceptual equivalent of the Xbase work area table. It serves as the conduit to provide access to database tables through the Borland Database Engine (which is the API provided by Delphi to handle all access to various data formats). Figure 6.1 shows the object inspector for a ***TTable*** object.

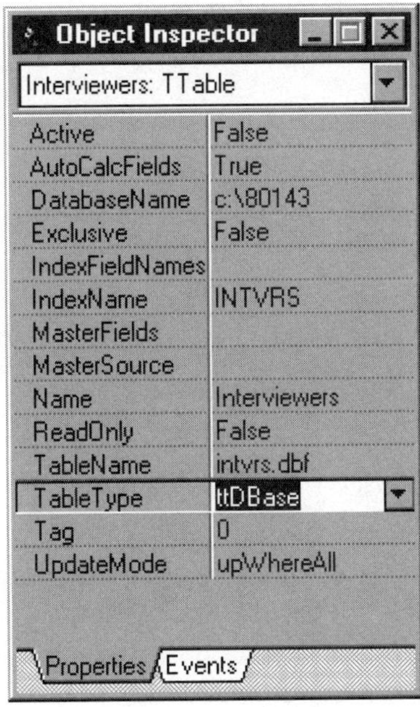

Figure 6.1 Object Inspector for TTable.

To use a **TTable** object for a DBF file, updating of certain property values is required so the object can find the DBF file.

DatabaseName Property

This property is a character field that contains the directory name where the desired DBF file resides.

TableName Property

This property contains the actual name of the desired DBF file.

TableType Property

This property indicates the type of table from a list of possible choices. Delphi is not limited to dBASE files, but can also access Paradox tables and ASCII text files. In addition, an object called **TQuery** operates similarly to **TTable**, but provides access to files stored in a client server environment.

Active Property

Once the object can find the table, set this property to True to allow the program to start working with the table. In Delphi's visual design tools, this will allow designing using actual data from the table.

Exclusive Property

This property contains a logical value that indicates whether or not you want exclusive use of the DBF file is desired.

Readonly Property

A logical value that indicates whether the file should be open for read-only access or for full read/write capabilities.

Visual Basic's Data Control

Visual Basic's **Data** control is its conceptual equivalent of the Xbase work area table. It serves as the conduit to provide access to database tables of a variety of types, including DBF files, spreadsheets, Access databases, Paradox files, and ASCII text files. Figure 6.2 shows the property inspector for a Data control.

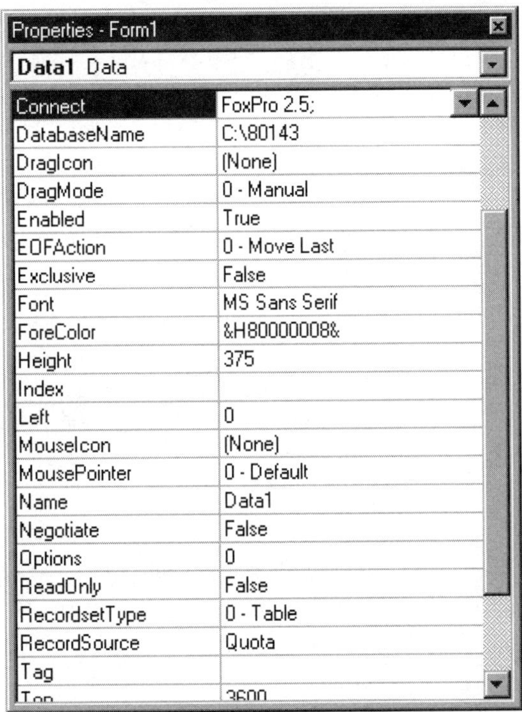

Figure 6.2 Visual Basic Data control.

To use a **Data** control for a DBF file, you need to update certain property values so the control can find the DBF file.

DatabaseName Property

This character field is the directory path where the DBF file is located.

Connect Property

This entry from a list of possible choices indicates the type of data we want to access. Visual Basic is not limited to dBASE files only, but can also access spreadsheets, Access tables, Paradox tables, and ASCII text files.

It is important to know about the DBF file and which indexes you are using. FoxPro, dBASE IV, and Clipper all have slight variations to the basic DBF structure and to the index files. Visual Basic needs to know whether the data source and associated indexes are from dBASE III, dBASE IV, dBASE 5, FoxPro 2.0, FoxPro 2.5, or FoxPro 3.0. Visual Basic cannot directly work with NTX files from Clipper.

RecordSource Property

This entry contains the actual name of the DBF file we want to use. The value you specify in the **Connect** property will help determine files and file extensions that could be used as a **RecordSource.** If you specify some Excel variation, then only XLS files will be valid candidates to use as the **RecordSource.**

RecordSet Property

This object, which is a property of the table object, controls the control record within the table. It is automatically created whenever a data control is created. It has its own set of methods and properties that supplement those of the data control.

Enabled Property

Once the control has been told where to find the table, this property can be set to True to allow the program to access its data.

Exclusive Property

A logical value that indicates whether or not exclusive use of the DBF file is desired.

Readonly Property

A logical value that indicates whether the file should be open for read-only access or for full read/write capabilities.

Visual Basic Databases

Visual Basic handles DBF files differently than XBase languages do. Although there are counterparts in Visual Basic to most of the Xbase commands and functions, it is worth reviewing Visual Basic's view of a database.

Database Object

The *Database* object is the primary tool used to manipulate data with a data file in Visual Basic. The database object, however, contains much more than simply rows and fields. The other objects it contains are:

1. **TableDef** object—properties and methods pertaining to the data storage itself. Field information and index file information is found within the **TableDef** object (of the **Database** object).
2. **Relations** object—properties and methods dealing with relationship between one or more tables.
3. **RecordSet** object—information about the records and record pointer in a table. Information such as **BOF()**, **EOF()**, and filters are controlled through this object.

Many of the Xbase commands that we use will be done by creating new objects and attaching them to the database object. For example, setting relationships will require building a **Relations** object and then adding it to the **Database** object. Creating index files will work in a similar manner.

Xbase Work Area Commands and Functions

Most of the Xbase work area commands and functions you've become familiar with are available in both Delphi and Visual Basic. However, some are more intuitive and obvious than others. Remember that most of the commands can be found as methods to the objects and most of the functions as object property values.

This section looks at some of the Xbase commands and functions and explores how to perform the same functionality in Delphi and Visual Basic.

Opening DBF Files

In Xbase, a large work area table is automatically set up. In Delphi and VB, the objects need to be created at design time, because a number of empty objects will not be automatically created. Your USE commands in Xbase will need to be replaced by creating objects in the visual design tools.

The syntax for Xbase's use command is:

```
USE <filename>     [ ALIAS <alias_name> ] [EXCLUSIVE | SHARED]
      [ NO UPDATE (FoxPro)  or READONLY (Clipper) ]
      [VIA 'Driver' (Clipper) ]
```

Most of the keyword modifiers are optional, with reasonable default values set for them.

<filename>

In Xbase, you specify the fully qualified file name, e.g., C:\80143\INTVRS.DBF. In Delphi and VB you need to place the path into the **DatabaseName** property and the file name into the **TableName** (Delphi) or **RecordSource** (Visual Basic) property. You will also need to set the **Active** (Delphi) or **Enabled** (Visual Basic) flag to True, since Xbase's USE command automatically enables the file.

ALIAS <aliasname>

The **ALIAS** keyword allows you to assign a different identifier for referring to the work area. If you don't specify the alias, the default is the file name. This is similar to the **name** property in Delphi and Visual Basic, except that the default names tend to be less meaningful (i.e., TABLE1 and DATA1). At design time, be sure to assign a value to the name property that will allow the code to clearly indicate which file is being worked with.

EXCLUSIVE | SHARED

This keyword to the USE command is the same as the **Exclusive** property. Set **Exclusive** to True if using the exclusive keyword or set it to False if you are using the SHARED keyword.

NO UPDATE | READONLY

This keyword, if present, causes the file to be opened for read-only access to the data. Set the **Readonly** property to True if you need read-only access to files. The default setting is False.

VIA <driver>

This keyword, available only in Clipper, specifies the data type that is being manipulated in the work area. Although a few special drivers are available, this keyword mostly informs Clipper which indexing scheme should be used. (DBFMDX-dbase IV and 5 files, DBFCDX-FoxPro compatible files, DBFNTX-Clipper's own driver.)

In Visual Basic, the **Connect** property allows you to specify either dBASE files and indices or FoxPro files and indices. There is no support for NTX files.

In Delphi, the **TableType** property specifies the type of data, but for DBF files, it only works with MDX indexes from dBASE. A product called Apollo, from Successware, Inc., allows access FoxPro compatible indices (i.e., CDX files) from Delphi. With Apollo, the number of choices for the TableType property will be increased to include FoxPro as well as some custom index drivers from Successware. If you want to use Delphi to access FoxPro compatible indices, consider using Apollo.

Closing DBF Files

If the USE command is used without any parameters in Xbase, then the file in the current work area is closed and the work area is emptied. The same result is achieved in Delphi by setting the object's **Active** property to False, and in Visual Basic by setting the **Enabled** property to False.

Xbase keeps 250 work areas available while in Delphi and Visual Basic. It is the programmer's responsibility to create and free the database objects as needed. The concept of implicitly closing a file by opening a new file in the same work area is not appropriate in the object-oriented world of Visual Basic and Delphi. There aren't any predefined objects just waiting for a database, rather the objects must be created as needed. Once the file is closed, the object is freed rather than kept waiting for another file.

Specifying Indexes and Relations

DBF files are typically arranged in the order they are entered, the earliest records are towards the beginning of the file and the later records and towards the end. The record number could be thought of as a unique key which allows you to access records. Of course, sequential entry, or natural order as it is called, is not exactly the most useful order. Most DBF files will have attached with it an index file that provides one or more alternative orders, based upon index keys. Index keys are fields or expressions that should be used to determine the logical view of the database.

The index files themselves provide an ordering scheme to the database. Some techniques, such as FoxPro's Rushmore, use the index file to speed up database searching and filtering. Index files can contain a single index expression or can be a tagged index, which contains multiple expressions in single file. There are many different varieties of index file structure, although the most common are:

NTX, IDX, NDX	Clipper, FoxPro, dBASE III single entry index files
CDX, MDX	FoxPro, dBASE IV and V multiple tag index files

SET INDEX TO

The **SET INDEX TO** command specifies the name of a file that should be used as an index for the current work area. With the tagged index files, it is not necessary to specify the index name, because it is automatically opened when the database file is opened.

Because Delphi supports only the tagged indices, it automatically opens the index file when the table is made active. There is no need to specify an additional existing index name, although indexes may need to be created during your program.

Specifying additional indices in Visual Basic requires creating an INF file with the same name as the DBF file and placing the file in the same directory as the DBF file. Each entry in the INF file contains an index number (using the identifiers CDXn or IDXn) and an index file name (e.g., LastName.CDX). The entries are preceded by a source database type. For example, the INF file for a FoxPro 2.0 table named Authors would be named Authors.INF, and could contain the following entries.

```
[FoxPro 2.0]
CDX1=AuthorID.CDX
CDX2=LastName.CDX
CDX3=Zip.CDX
```

Once connected to this table, Visual Basic will open the index specified in the INF file and you can access them through the index name property.

SET ORDER TO

Once an index is opened in Xbase, the **Set Order To** command is used to switch between different index keys. Its syntax is:

```
SET ORDER  TO [ <number>  | TAG <tag_name> ]
```

where **<number>** can be the tag at the associated position in the list of all tags. The **<tag_name>** option is used to specify the tag by name, rather than position. You should use the **<tag_name>** variation whenever possible because it makes more readable code and also is more compatible with VB and Delphi, which don't support set index order by number.

To switch index orders in Delphi or Visual Basic, the value of the **Indexname** property must be changed. If this property is blank, the default order for the file is natural or record number order. If not blank, the property value must be one of the existing tag names in the index file. In Visual Basic, the indexname property is found in the **RecordSet** property of the data control, while in Delphi it is a property of the **TTable** object.

The three methods for specifying an index order are compared below:

```
XBASE -  select customer
         set order to tag id_code

Delphi-  customer.indexname := 'id_code' ;

VB    -  customer.recordset.index = "id_code"
```

INDEX

The **INDEX** command creates a file or adds a tag to an existing file. The file or tag will contain a set of keyed pairs, consisting of an expression, which is often a list of fields, and a record number. The index can then be used to impose a logical ordering upon a DBF file. The Xbase syntax for the INDEX command is:

```
INDEX ON <expression> [TAG <tag_name> | TO <filename> ]
         [UNIQUE] [ ASCENDING | DESCENDING ]
```

where the **<expression>** is any valid Xbase expression. However, it is strongly recommend that you leave this to combination of fields, rather than a using defined function as allowed by some variations of Xbase. If your index keys rely on UDF()s, then it will be very difficult to scale the application to a client/server platform which does not support user-defined functions in index expressions. If you rely on the function, then add a field to the database that will hold the result of the function and create an index on that field.

The **<tag_name>** specifies the tag name to add to or update in an existing index file. You can also index into a separate index file by specifying the **<filename>** syntax.

The **UNIQUE** keyword, if present, writes only the first unique occurrence of the index key into the index, all other database records will be invisible when using this index view. If **UNIQUE** is not specified, every record, even duplicates, will have a record in the index file.

ASCENDING or **DESCENDING** specifies the sequence of keyed pairs in the order. If neither clause is specified, the default is ASCENDING.

In Delphi, the **AddIndex** method creates a new index for the tTable. Its syntax is:

```
AddIndex( <name>, <field_list>, <options> )
```

where **<name>** is the name of the new index tag, **<field_list>** is a list of the fields to include in the index, with multiple fields separated by a semicolon, and**<options>** is a set of values which can include the following:

ixUnique	Unique keys only, like the **UNIQUE** keyword
ixDescending	Descending order on the index
ixCaseInsensitive	Forces the fields to be a consistent case in the index
ixExpression	Allows you to create indexes based on expressions, rather than just columns

Note that an index created using ixExpression will not easily port to an SQL-based server application.

The following Delphi code fragment creates an index on customer number and name. It is a unique index that is case insensitive, i.e., similar to using upper() or lower() in Xbase.

```
Customer.AddIndex('Cust', 'CustNo;CustName' [ixUnique,
ixCaseInsensitive])
```

In Visual Basic, index creation is slightly more complex, but not much. The first method you need to call is the **CreateIndex**() method of the data control. This will create an index object with its own properties and methods. Its syntax is:

```
variable  = CreateIndex( "Name" )
```

where **<name>** is the tag name you wish to create. The variable will hold an index object, which has its own set of properties and methods. The **CreateField**() method of the created index object can be used to specify the field you want to index on. The index object also has a **Unique** property if this is required by the program.

The following code fragment creates a customer number index in Visual Basic:

```
DIM MyIndexAS     Index
DIM MyFieldAS     Field
Set MyIndex = MyTableDef.CreateIndex ("CustNo")
Set MyField = MyIndex.CreateField ("CustNumber")

MyIndex.Primary = False
MyIndex.Unique = True
MyIndex.Fields.Append MyField
```

Once the new index is created and the property values are set, this index can be added to the **Index** property of the Recordset data control. Visual Basic provides a good deal of flexibility in the level of control it provides, but, as you can see from the examples above, some operations that are one-line commands in Xbase require a few more lines in Visual Basic.

SET RELATION TO

The ***SET RELATION To*** command links two files together in a parent and child relationship. A relation causes the record pointer to move in the child work area in accordance with the movement of the record pointer in the parent work area. If no match is found in the child work area, the child record pointer is positioned at the end of the file. Its syntax is:

```
SET RELATION TO [<expKey> | <nRecord> INTO <xcAlias>]
```

where **<expKey>** is an expression, usually a field name, that performs a SEEK in the child work area each time the record pointer moves in the parent work area. For this to work, the child work area must have an index in USE.

<nRecord> is a numeric expression that performs a GOTO to the matching record number in the child work area each time the record pointer moves in the parent work area. **INTO <xcAlias>** identifies the child work area.

Setting a relation in Delphi is accomplished by specifying values in two properties in the table object. The **MasterSource** property is a reference to the table you want to relation the current table to. The **MasterFields** property is used to specify the column(s) to link a detail table with a master table that is specified by the **MasterSource** property. **MasterFields** is a string consisting of one or more column names that join the two tables. Separate multiple column names with semicolons. Each time the current record in the master table changes, the new values in those fields are used to select corresponding records from the detail table for display.

NOTE

One of the objects not yet discussed for Delphi is the **Datasource**. A **Datasource** object is primarily a linkage between tables and controls. We will discuss the object later in this chapter in the section on controls. However, the **Datasource** object is used when setting relations rather than linking the two table objects directly. Typically all table objects will have a corresponding **Datasource** object to handle linkages.

In Visual Basic, a relationship object is created by using the **CreateRelation** method of the **Database** object. This object should be saved to a variable so that you can manipulate its properties. Once the relationship is created, the **Table** property variable should be set to the name of the parent database and the **ForeignTable** should be set to the name of the child database.

The **CreateField** method is then called to specify the field that should be used to link the two tables. Listing 6.1 shows the Visual Basic code used to create and update the relation object.

Listing 6.1 Code to create relation objects.

```
Set RelObject = Dbfobject.CreateRelation("Id_code")
 RelObject.Table        = "Customer"
 RelObject.ForeignTable = "Invoices"
 RelObject.Attributes   = 0
Set Fldobject = Relobject.CreateField("Cust_id")
 Fldobject.ForeignName = "CustomerId"

 Relobject.Fields.Append Fldobject
 Dbfobject.Relations.Append Relobject
```

Basic Navigation Commands

Xbase grants total control over the current record in the work area at all times. You can freely navigate through the work area to position the data at any record and the work area table will stay current. The record pointer is a numeric value that indicates which record you are currently positioned on. In Delphi and Visual Basic terminology speak, the record pointer is called the cursor.

In this section, we will explore the equivalent Delphi/Visual Basic commands to move the record pointer/cursor all over the place.

GO TOP

The **GO TOP** command from Xbase moves the pointer to the very first logical record in the DBF file. A logical record indicates the record that is first in the index, as opposed to the physical record, which is that actual record in the DBF file itself. In addition, if any changes were made to the current record, the changes will be written back to the disk before the record pointer is moved.

The **First** (Delphi) / **MoveFirst** (Visual Basic) method moves the cursor to the first logical record in the file, as defined by the current index. In Visual Basic, the **MoveFirst** method is applied to the **Record Set** component of the data control.

GO BOTTOM

The **GO BOTTOM** command from Xbase moves the pointer to the very last logical record in the DBF file. In addition, if any changes were made to the current record, the changes will be written back to the disk before the record pointer is moved.

The **Last** (Delphi) / **MoveLast** (Visual Basic) method moves the cursor to the last logical record in the file, as defined by the current index. In Visual Basic, the **MoveLast** method is applied to the **RecordSet** component of the data control.

SKIP

The ***SKIP*** command from Xbase moves the pointer forward or backwards the indicated number of records in the DBF file. If any changes were made to the current record, the changes will be written back to the disk before the record pointer is moved.

SKIP is followed by a numeric value indicating the number of records to move. A positive value means to move forwards, towards the end of the file, while a negative number means to move backwards, towards the beginning of the file.

The **Next** (Delphi) / **MoveNext** (Visual Basic) method moves the cursor one record in the forward direction, as defined by the current index. The **Prior** (Delphi) / **MovePrevious** (Visual Basic) method moves the cursor one record in the backwards direction. In Visual Basic, the **MoveNext** and **MovePrevious** methods are applied to the **RecordSet** component of the data control.

GOTO

In Xbase, you can move to any specific record number by using the **GOTO** command. Its syntax is:

```
GOTO <number>
```

where **<number>** is the record number to move to. This is also the record number in physical order, regardless of the current index order. It is not a logical record number and record one in physical order is probably not the same as the go top command in indexed order.

Both Delphi and Visual Basic allow you to move to specific record numbers using a bookmark. A bookmark is used just like the record number in Xbase, although it is not only a numeric value, but rather a special structure for database movement.

In Delphi, there are three methods to the table object that are use for bookmarks. These methods are:

GetBookmark	allocates memory to set a bookmark at the current location.
GoToBookmark	navigates to the specified bookmark.
FreeBookmark	releases memory allocated for the specified bookmark

The methods are used together. The **GetBookmark**() method sets the bookmark to the current record and returns a variable. When passing the variable to the **GoToBookmark**() method, Delphi returns to the record number specified. When you are done using the bookmark, call **FreeBookmark** before reusing a bookmark or exiting the program.

In Visual Basic, **Bookmark** is a property of the **RecordSet** component of the data control. You may copy this property value into a string variable to save the current record number. You can return to that record number by setting the bookmark's property value to the contents of the variable.

Record Movement Example

Listing 6.2 is an example that shows the Visual Basic code to perform various record movements when the user clicks on command buttons.

Listing 6.2 Record movement in Visual Basic.

```
Private Sub GoTop_Click()
    QBASE.Recordset.MoveFirst      ' GO TOP commmand
End Sub

Private Sub GoBottom_Click()
    QBASE.Recordset.MoveLast       ' GO BOTTOM commmand
End Sub

Private Sub Next_Click()
    QBASE.Recordset.MoveNext       ' SKIP +1 commmand
```

```
End Sub

Private Sub Prior_Click()
    QBASE.Recordset.MovePrevious  ' SKIP -1 commmand
End Sub
```

Finding Data

Often in database applications, users want to find a particular record for display or edit purpose. Xbase provides two commands to search for data, depending upon the needs and presence of indexes. Of course, both commands can be emulated in Visual Basic and Delphi.

SEEK

The **SEEK** command searches the controlling index order for the first key value until a match is found. If there is a match, the record pointer is positioned to the record found in the order. Its basic syntax is:

```
SEEK <expression>
```

where **<expression>** matches the data that is in the index key. If the index is built on a numeric field, then expression should be a number.

Most Xbase variations have enhanced the seek commands, most notably by providing a **Set Softseek** (Clipper) or **Set Near** (FoxPro) capability, that causes the seek not to find an exact match, but rather the closest matching record. In addition, there is the ability to find the last occurrence of a particular key, rather than the first occurrence of the key. (Adding the **LAST** keyword in Clipper or specifying **DESCENDING** in FoxPro).

In Delphi, the **FindKey** and **FindNearest** methods of the table object allow you to seek matching records based upon index keys. The **FindKey** method searches the database table to find a record whose index fields match those passed as an argument to the method. **FindKey** takes a comma-delimited array of values as its argument, where each value corresponds to a index column in the underlying table.

If **FindKey** finds the record in the table, it moves the cursor there, and returns True. If a matching record is not found, it does not move the cursor, and returns False.

FindNearest finds the closest matching record to the specified key values. (Similar to FoxPro's **Set Near** or Clipper's **Set Softseek**). It operates similar to **FindKey**, except that it returns a close match, not necessarily an exact match. Listing 6.3 shows some Delphi code to illustrate the **Find** methods

Listing 6.3 FindKey() and FindNearest().

```
{ Search for CustNo = '1234' }
if Customer.FindKey(['1234']) then
   ShowMessage('Customer Found')
else
   { Search for CustNo >= '1234' }
  Customer.FindNearest(['1234']) ;
```

In Visual Basic, you use the **SEEK** method of the **RecordSet** object. Its syntax is

```
SEEK <comparison>,< key1>,<key2>
```

where **<comparison>** is a string expressions of : "<", "<=", "=", ">=", or ">", and **<key1>, <key2>** are values that correspond to the index's key values.

The SEEK method searches through the specified key fields and locates the first record that matches the criteria specified. Once found, it makes that record current and the **NoMatch** property is set to FALSE. If not found, then the **NoMatch** property is set to True.

If you use "=" for comparison, then the first matching record is found. ">=" finds the first matching record or the one after it and ">" finds the first record after the matching record. These comparison operators allow you to emulate the **Softseek** and **Near** commands from Xbase. If comparison is "<" or "<=", SEEK starts at the end of the index and searches backward, similarly to the LAST /DESCENDING options from Xbase.

Listing 6.4 shows Visual Basic code used to seek a particular customer in the id_code index order.

Listing 6.4 Seeking in Visual Basic.

```
Customer.Index = "ID_CODE"        ' Define current index.
Customer.Seek "=", "1234"         ' Seek record.
If Customer.NoMatch Then...       ' Record was not found
```

Be sure to check the value of the **NoMatch** property after a seek operation, similar to checking the **FOUND** or **EOF** functions in Xbase.

LOCATE

The **LOCATE** command searches for the first record in the current work area that matches the specified conditions and scope. When you first execute a **LOCATE**, it searches from the beginning record of the scope for the first matching record in the current work area. It terminates when a match is found or the end of the **LOCATE** scope is reached. If it is successful, the matching record becomes the current record and **FOUND** returns True. If it is unsuccessful, **FOUND** returns False.

LOCATE works with CONTINUE. Once a LOCATE has been issued, you can resume the search from the current record pointer position with CONTINUE.

In Delphi, the **SetKey, GoToKey,** and **GoToNearest** methods of the table object provide similar functionality to the locate command. However, keep in mind that Delphi works almost exclusively from the index keys. While these methods let you move the record pointer based upon multiple field conditions, it is still expected that the field values exist in the index. To emulate a **LOCATE** command directly against database fields, you would need to write code to skip through the database and do comparisons directly. Or, once you are more comfortable with Delphi, you could consider using SQL statements and the **tQuery** object rather than the **tTable** object. Of course, converting an Xbase application directly to a SQL based program is more involved than what is covered in this book.

The **SetKey**() method places the database table into a searchable state called **SetKey** state. While in this state, field values you write into the buffer (work area) are not intended for database update, but rather for searching. Listing 6.5 shows an example of loading the fields for a search operation.

Listing 6.5 Writing Field Values for Searching.

```
with customer do
  begin
   SetKey;
   FieldByName('State').AsString := 'CA';
   FieldByName('City').AsString := 'Scotts Valley';
   GotoKey;
  end;
```

Once the fields you want to search for are loaded, you can do the **GoToKey** method to find the exact key or the **GoToNearest** method to find the closest matching record.

Locating a record in Visual Basic also relies upon SQL (Structured Query Language). If you plan on converting code that uses the **LOCATE** command heavily, you should learn basic SQL constructs. Both languages allow you to apply SQL queries to DBF files. Listing 6.6 shows a sample of some Visual Basic code to create an SQL query statement and use it to find certain records in the vendor's database file.

Listing 6.6 SQL with Visual Basic.

```
Dimension SQL$ as String

SQL$ = "Select * FROM Vendors WHERE Terms = 'C.O.D.' "
' Open recordset.
Set SubSet = Vendor.OpenRecordset(SQL$, dbOpenDynaset)
Do Until SubSet.EOF                          ' Begin loop.
 SubSet.Edit                                 ' Enable editing.
 SubSet.Title = "Net 30"                     ' Change terms.
 Subset.Update                               ' Save changes.
 Subset.MoveNext                             ' CONTINUE command
Loop

Subset.Close                                 ' Close table.
Vendors.Close
```

Editing Commands

Xbase's editing commands allow changes to be made to the records in the database. You can add and delete records, and change the contents of individual fields. In addition, records which have been tagged for deletion can be physically removed from the file. Finally, all of the records can be removed to create a completely empty dataset.

APPEND BLANK

The **APPEND BLANK** command adds a new record to the end of the current database file and then makes it the current record. The new field values are initialized to the empty values for each data type: character fields are assigned with spaces; numeric fields are assigned zero; logical fields are assigned false (.F.); date fields are assigned CTOD(" "); and memo fields are left empty.

The **Append** method (Delphi) on the **Table** object or the **AddNew** method (Visual Basic) on the **RecordSet** component of a data control object, moves the cursor to the end of the dataset and opens a new, empty record. It is marked as the current record and can be edited by the user.

COMMIT

COMMIT is a database command that flushes buffers and performs a solid-disk write for all work areas with open database and index files. The solid-disk write capability is available under DOS version 3.3 and above. Under DOS 3.2 or less, **COMMIT** flushes Clipper buffers to DOS.

The **Post**() method (Delphi) / **Update**() method (Visual Basic) writes the current record to the database. Posting can be done explicitly, or implicitly as part of another procedure. When an application moves off the current record, the post method is called implicitly.

DELETE

DELETE is a database command that tags records so they can be filtered with **SET DELETED ON**, queried with **DELETED**, or physically removed from the database file with **PACK**. In addition, display commands such as **LIST** and **DISPLAY** identify deleted records with an asterisk (*) character. Once records are deleted, you can reinstate them by using **RECALL**. If you want to remove all records from a database file, use **ZAP** instead of **DELETE ALL** and **PACK**.

The **Delete** method (in both Delphi and Visual Basic) deletes the current record from the dataset. The next record then becomes the new current record. If the record deleted was the last record in the dataset, then the previous record becomes the current record.

REPLACE

The **REPLACE** command in Xbase allows fields to be updated in a database. Its syntax is simply:

```
REPLACE <field_name> with <value>
```

The contents of the field in the work area is updated with the new value. When the changes are committed to disk, either implicitly by moving to a new record or by explicitly issuing a command, the work area field values are written to the DBF file on the disk.

In Delphi field values are changed using the **FieldbyName** method of the table object. The method returns a pointer to field specified. You can then replace the field's value using the pointer. For example, the Xbase code:

```
replace id_code with "PECO-NJ"
```

would be written in Delphi as:

```
customer.Edit;
customer.fieldbyName('ID_CODE').asString := 'PECO-NJ' ;
customer.Post;
```

In Visual Basic, you must first issue the **Edit** method to the record set before you can update the fields. The fields are specified directly by field name as you can assign variables of the property type directly to the field names. Once you've updated the fields, you need to call the **Update** method to post the field changes to the DBF file. For example, to update the customer id code in Visual Basic:

```
Customer.Edit                        ' Enable editing.
Customer!Id_code = "PECO-NJ"         ' Change terms.
Customer.Update                      ' Save changes.
```

ZAP

The **ZAP** command permanently removes all records from files open in the current work area. This includes the current database file, index files, and associated memo file. Disk space previously occupied by the ZAPped files is released to the operating system.

The **EmptyTable** method in Delphi deletes all records from the database table. Before calling this method, the **DatabaseName**, **TableName** and **TableType** properties must all be assigned values. If the table is open, it must have been opened with the **Exclusive** property set to True. In Visual Basic, you need to use the SQL command "DELETE *" to remove all the records from a DBF file.

Data Filtering

It is often useful to view only a subset of records in a database file. In Xbase, this process is called filtering, where only records meeting a particular condition are visible. Originally many Xbase programmers moved away from relying on **SET FILTER TO** since its performance was not very impressive. However, with Rushmore technology in FoxPro and Clipmore technology in Clipper, filtering has become a very useful command in many Xbase applications.

SET FILTER TO

The **SET FILTER TO** command causes the current work area to act as if it contains only the records that match the specified condition. The filter condition is one of the properties of a work area. Its syntax is:

```
SET FILTER TO <condition>
```

Most commands and functions that move the record pointer honor the current filter with the exception of those commands that access records by record number, such as the **GOTO** command. Once a filter is set, it is not activated until the record pointer is moved from its current position. You can use **GO TOP** to activate the filter.

The **SetRange** method (in Delphi) of the table object provides the functionality of Xbase's filter command. Its syntax is:

```
SetRange( aStartValues, aEndValues )
```

SetRange assigns the elements of **StartValues** to the beginning index key, the elements of EndValues to the ending index key, and then calls **ApplyRange**. This enables an application to filter the data visible to the dataset. The **SetRange** method works only with indexed fields. If you need to filter data based upon non indexed fields, you must use the SQL statements against the open DBF file.

To set a filter condition in Visual Basic, create a string containing a valid SQL statement and assign this string to the **Filter** property of the **RecordSet** component. Once you've created a filter condition, you need to open a subset of the **RecordSet** by using the **OpenRecordSet** function as illustrated below:

```
Customer.Filter = "[State] = 'PA'"                ' Set filter condition.
Set FiltCustomers = Customer.OpenRecordset()      ' Create filtered view.
```

Data Aware Controls

Although the properties and methods provided in Delphi and Visual Basic to emulate most of Xbase's functionality have been discussed, one aspect that must be considered is that of controls that are tied to a database. These are standard controls, much like we explored in Chapter 4, with a small difference—the values in these controls come directly from fields within an associated database file. Any changes made in these controls will update fields in the database and, as the record pointer is moved, the contents of the controls will change.

Linking Controls with a Database

In order for a control to be made *data aware*, the control must be associated with a data source and must know which field should be used to provide the value for the control. Delphi and Visual Basic handle the issue of data aware controls slightly differently.

Data Aware Controls in Delphi

Delphi's component palette lists a separate tab of controls that are data aware. These are the same as the basic editing controls with additional properties to link them to a **Datasource**. However, the **Datasource** is not the same as the **Table** object in Delphi. The **Datasource** is an object in Delphi that has a sole purpose to link table objects to controls. Figure 6.3 illustrates the relationship between the table object, the **Datasource** object, and data aware controls.

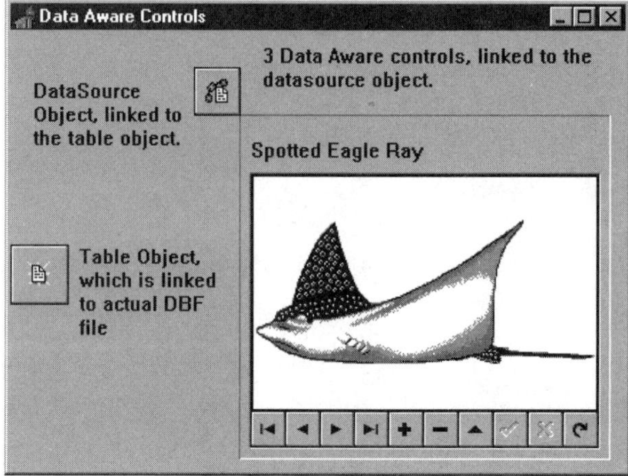

Figure 6.3 Relationship between table, datasource, and controls.

The **Datasource** object has only a few properties, but the most important one is the ***dataset*** property which specifies the name of the table or query object that this **Datasource** is attached. For the most part, every time a **Table** or **Query** object is created, you will create an associated **Datasource** object should be created.

Once the **Datasource** object is created and set to the proper table, you can place controls on the forms. Delphi provides the following data aware controls.

dbText	Similar to the label control
dbEdit	Similar to the edit control
dbMemo	Similar to the memo editing control
dbImage	Similar to the image control, except the image is stored in a memo field of the associated database
dbListBox	Similar to the list box control, where the choices are stored in the program
dbComboBox	Similar to the combo box control, choices embedded in code
dbCheckBox	Similar to the check box control
dbRadioGroup	Similar to radio buttons control
dbLookupList	List box, with choices stored in another database
dbLookupCombo	Combo box control, with choice stored in another database

Each of these controls has two additional properties; one is the **DataSource**, property which specifies the name of the **Datasource** object linked to this control. The other property is the **DataField** property which specified which field in the data source file is used to populate the control. By simply updating these fields after placing the control on the form, the control will now be updated as the record pointer is moved in the **Table** object.

Data Aware Controls in Visual Basic

Visual Basic does not have any special data aware controls, but rather each of its controls have properties that, if updated, cause the controls to be data aware. (Visual Basic uses the terminology bound controls interchangeably with data aware controls).

To bind a control to a field in a database at run-time, hence creating a data aware link, you must specify a **Data** control in the **DataSource** property at design time.

To complete the connection with the field in the **RecordSet** of the **Data** control, you must also provide the name of a **Field** object in the *DataField* property. Unlike the **DataField** property, the **DataSource** property setting isn't available at run-time.

Browsing

One of the more powerful abilities in Xbase languages is that of browsing a table. From the simple **BROWSE** command in dBASE III to the complex **Tbrowse** object of Clipper, browsing DBF data in a row/column grid layout has long been one of the staples of the Xbase languages. The original dBASE III syntax for browse is:

```
BROWSE [FIELDS <list>] [LOCK <number of columns>]
[WIDTH <width> ]
```

You could simply issue a **BROWSE** and display all of the columns in the table or you could specify a list of fields to browse. You can also **LOCK** the number of column on the left most side to stay as the other column browse horizontally. The **<width>** specified the width of characters fields for editing purposes.

FoxPro Browsing

FoxPro's **Browse** command is a very powerful command that greatly enhances the original dBASE syntax. Its syntax is:

```
BROWSE   [FIELDS FieldList]       [FONT cFontName [, nFontSize]]
    [STYLE cFontStyle]     [FOR lExpression1 [REST]]
    [FORMAT]               [FREEZE FieldName]
    [KEY eExpression1 [, eExpression2]]
    [LAST | NOINIT]        [LOCK nNumberOfFields]
    [LPARTITION]   [NAME ObjectName]
    [NOAPPEND]     [NOCLEAR]
    [NODELETE]             [NOEDIT | NOMODIFY]
    [NOLGRID] [NORGRID]
    [NOLINK]
    [NOMENU]               [NOOPTIMIZE]
    [NOREFRESH]    [NORMAL]
    [NOWAIT]               [PARTITION nColumnNumber [LEDIT] [REDIT]]
    [PREFERENCE PreferenceName]   [SAVE]
    [TIMEOUT nSeconds]     [TITLE cTitleText]
    [VALID [:F] lExpression2 [ERROR cMessageText]]
    [WHEN lExpression3]    [WIDTH nFieldWidth]
```

```
[[WINDOW WindowName1]
[IN [WINDOW] WindowName2 | IN SCREEN | IN MACDESKTOP]]
[COLOR SCHEME nSchemeNumber | COLOR ColorPairList]
```

With this large number of options, the rest of this book could easily be filled talking about FoxPro's browse command. Suffice to say however, than almost all of the functionality of FoxPro's **Browse** command is available in Delphi and/or Visual Basic.

Clipper's TBROWSE Object

Clipper took a different approach to providing browse capabilities within the language. Rather than create a new command and group of functions, Clipper introduced object orientation into 5.x and provided an object class to handle browsing. To create a working browse meant creating two objects, one for the browse itself and any number of column objects to be placed into a collection of columns in the original browse object.

Browsing in Delphi

The **DBGrid** component is a data aware component that enables you to view and edit all the records from a table in a browse-like format. To create the browse, you should place the **DBGrid** component on the form and set its **DataSource** property to the name of an existing **Datasource** object. Figure 6.4 shows a browse screen for a general ledger using the **DBGrid** object in Delphi.

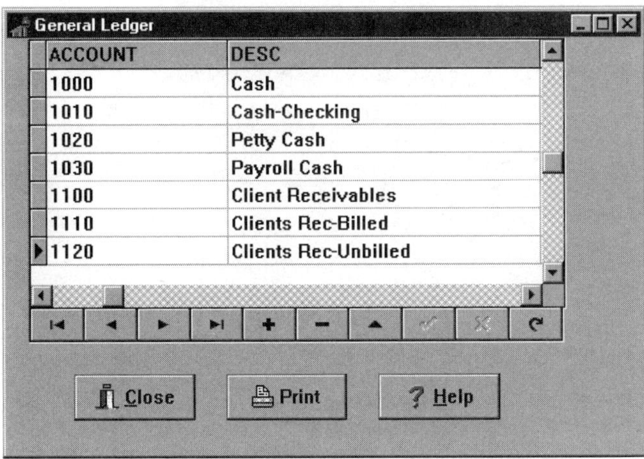

Figure 6.4 Browsing the general ledger.

There are a large number of properties and methods attached to the **DBGrid** component that allow you to customize much of the browsing mechanisms. Figure 6.5 shows the object inspector for a grid component to show some of the options available.

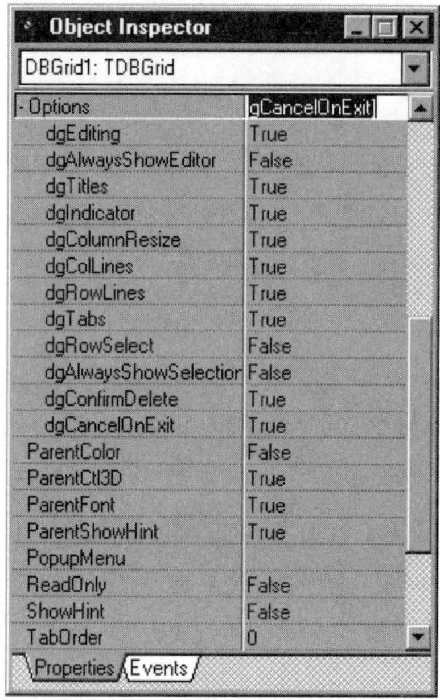

Figure 6.5 DBGrid options.

To control what fields appear in the grid component, edit the field list attached to the underlying table. By editing the field list, you can set field properties to invisible to exclude fields from the browse. Each field is a special object type in Delphi with properties that allow control of the display of data from the field, as well have input control over the field.

Browsing in Visual Basic

Visual Basic also has a **DBGrid** component which provides browse-like views of your database. Since the **DBGrid** is a data aware component, you need to set the **DataSource** property to an existing data control object. Once you've specified the data source, the browse will appear as shown in Figure 6.6.

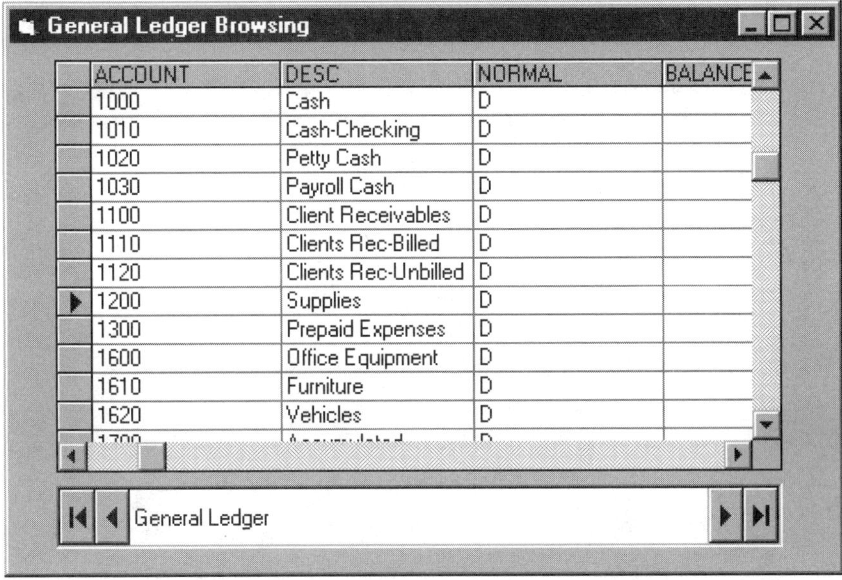

Figure 6.6 Chart of account browsing in Visual Basic.

Most of the display and editing abilities of the browse are controlled via the properties attached to the grid object. For example, the **AllowAddNew** property must be set to True to allow the user to add records into the grid. **AllowDelete** must be True for the user to be able to delete records while browsing, etc.

The **DBGrid** control contains a collection of column objects, which describe the fields to display in the grid. You can mark columns as visible, set their display font, etc. There are also column methods to allow you to retrieve text from the columns and write text back to the columns.

It's All There...

Although browsing databases is a strong feature of Xbase languages, both Delphi and Visual Basic provide equally rich objects to browse a dataset. While the syntax is different, the functionality is not. Anything you can browse in Xbase can be browsed in Delphi and Visual Basic as well. A good deal of the things you had to control in Xbase are handled easily by properties and methods in Delphi and VB.

Summary

Delphi and Visual Basic both provide the functionality that you use in Xbase, replacing the work area with an object to access the DBF file. With the large number of properties and methods on these objects, as well as the use of data aware (bound) controls, Delphi and Visual Basic allow you to easily manipulate DBF files just as easily as in Xbase languages.

CHAPTER 7:

WHEN IN ROME...

Although we can easily handle most DOS programming tasks in Windows, if that is all you do, you'll end up with a Windows program that acts like a DOS program. In this chapter, we will explore some of the common programming techniques in Windows that will allow your program to operate more like a Windows program than a DOS application ported to Windows.

Common Dialogs

Much of Windows' functionality is coded in run-time libraries stored in the \WINDOWS and \WINDOWS\SYSTEM directories. Your application code accesses these libraries at run-time for some functions, rather than imbedding all of the necessary library code into your executable file. When Windows 95 was introduced with a new appearance, it provided replacement run-time libraries but left the underlying API function calls the same. The result is that many applications which were written for Windows 3.1 immediately sported a new appearance when run under Windows 95.

The Windows API, which is accessible both to Delphi and Visual Basic, provides standard dialog boxes for some of the more common tasks used in a Windows application. This section explores these common dialog tasks, which should be used rather than writing your own for any tasks which can be accomplished with the dialog boxes. By relying upon the API calls, your program will share the interface look and feel from whichever version of Windows the user is running.

OpenDialog

The **OpenDialog** component creates a common Windows **OpenDialog** box that allows users to specify the name of a file to open. When a user enters a file name in an **OpenDialog** box, the file name is assigned to the **FileName** property of the object, which can be used to specify the desired file to open in the application code.

Figure 7.1 shows the **OpenDialog** component in Windows 95. Figure 7.2 shows the same component when run under Windows 3.1. Although they look different and have slight variations in how they operate, to the application code, the components look the same.

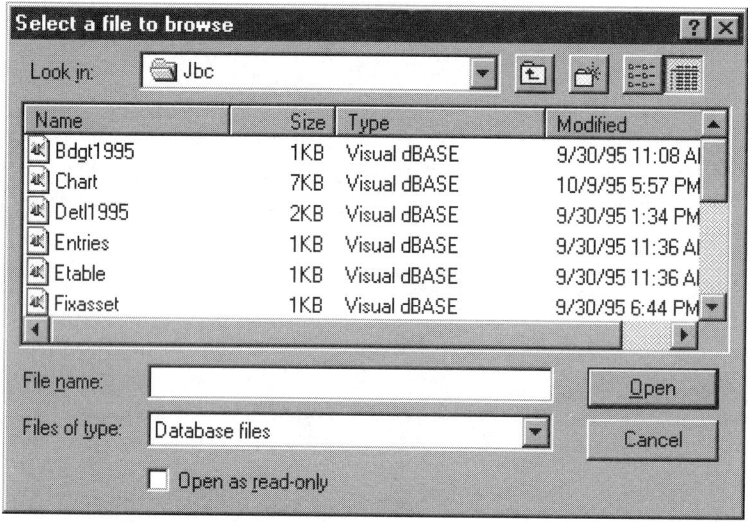

Figure 7.1 OpenDialog box—Windows 95.

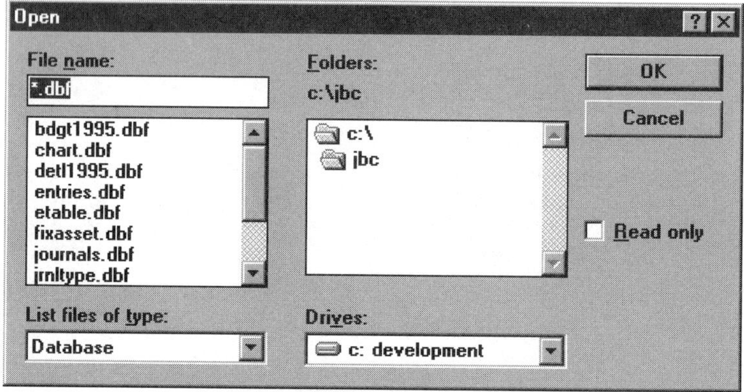

Figure 7.2 OpenDialog box—Windows 3.1.

Delphi and Visual Basic have slightly different approaches to handling the **OpenDialog** box and other common dialogs. In Delphi, each common dialog is a separate component that can be placed on the form. In Visual Basic, there is a common dialog object to use, with different methods depending upon which of the standard dialogs you wish to present the user. In both cases, the common dialog has to be placed on the form and assigned a name. This provides a way to access its properties and methods.

Setting Dialog Properties

There are a number of properties that can be set on the dialog object to control how it operates for the user. In general, set the properties first and then call the appropriate method to allow the user to work with the dialog box. When the user is done, extract the filename property (and any other properties) for use within the application.

Setting File Filters

The **Filter** property determines the file patterns available to the user to select which files to display in the dialog box's list box. A file filter, sometimes called a file mask, is a file name that usually includes wildcard characters (*.DBF, for example). Only files that match the selected file filter are displayed in the dialog box's list box, and the selected file filter appears in the File Name edit box.

Each mask in the filter property consists of two parts. The first is a descriptive name of the filter, such as Database, Indexes, and Spreadsheets. The second is the actual filter to apply, such as *.DBF, *.CDX, *.XLS. Each part is separated by the pipe character (ASCII 124). If you need multiple files, use another pipe character to separate them, for example:

```
Databases|*.DBF|Indexes|*.CDX|Spreadsheets|*.XLS,*.WK?
```

This example allows the user to select databases, indexes, or spreadsheets. The file type will be determined by the extension following the pipe character, i.e., databases are *.DBF, indexes are *.CDX, and spreadsheets are either *.XLS or *.WK.

Default File Extension

The **DefaultExt** property specifies the extension that is added to the file name if the user doesn't include a file name extension. If the user specifies an extension for the file name, the value of the **DefaultExt** property is ignored. If the **DefaultExt** value remains blank, no extension is added to the file name entered in the File Name edit box. The extension can be up to three characters and should not include the period.

Specifying the Current Directory

The **InitialDir** (Delphi) / **InitDir** (Visual Basic) property determines the current directory when the dialog box first appears and is shown as the current directory in the directory tree. Only files in the current directory appear in the dialog box's list box of file names.

When specifying the initial directory, include its full path name. For example:

```
C:\WINDOWS\SYSTEM
```

If no initial directory, or a directory that does not exist or cannot be accessed is specified, the directory that is current when the dialog box appears remains the current directory.

Changing the Title

The **Title** (Delphi) / **DialogTitle** (Visual Basic) property determines the text that appears in the dialog box's title bar.

Other Options

There are a large number of additional settings available. For example, read-only files can be excluded from display and from being selected, the user can be prevented from changing directories, multiple file selections can be allowed, etc. By setting the proper options, you should be able to use the **OpenDialog** box at any time to bring a file in from the disk. In Delphi, these additional options are stored in the **Options** property and in Visual Basic they are stored in the **flags** property.

Calling the Dialog Box

After all of the properties are specified, control needs to passed to the dialog box. In Delphi, this is done by using the **Execute** method of the particular dialog box. In Visual Basic, you need to call the **ShowOpen()** method to invoke the file common dialog box. Once control is returned to your application from the dialog box, you can extract the various property values, most notably **Filename**, from the dialog box for use in the application. In Visual Basic, the **Filetitle** property extracts just the file name portion while **InitDir** is updated to contain the file's directory.

Listing 7.1 shows some Visual Basic code used to call the common dialog's open method and extract the path and file name which are placed into the appropriate properties of a data control.

Listing 7.1 Visual Basic using common dialog.

```
Private Sub Form_Load()
    CommonDlg.ShowOpen              ' Show the open dialog window
    BrowseFile.DatabaseName = CommonStuff.InitDir ' Extract path
    BrowseFile.RecordSource = CommonStuff.FileTitle
End Sub
```

Listing 7.2 shows an example from Delphi where the user can select multiple files, possibly for backup purposes. This example calls the open dialog component allowing the user to select files. Once selected, the program transfers these files into a listbox controls for processing.

Listing 7.2 Delphi OpenDialog example.

```
begin
  OpenDialog1.Options := [ofAllowMultiSelect];
  OpenDialog1.Filter := 'All files (*.*)|*.*';
   if OpenDialog1.Execute then
       ListBox1.Items := OpenDialog1.Files;
end;
```

SaveDialog

The **SaveDialog** component will create a common Windows **SaveDialog** box that allows users to specify the name of a file to save. When a user enters a file name in a **SaveDialog** box, the file name is assigned to the FileName property of the object. You can then use this property value to specify the file you want to save.

Figure 7.3 shows the **SaveDialog** component at work. Figure 7.4 shows the Windows 3.1 version of the same dialog box.

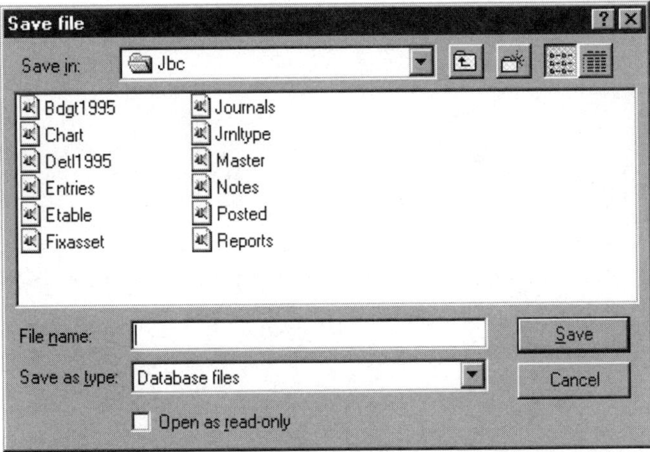

Figure 7.3 SaveDialog box—Windows 95 style.

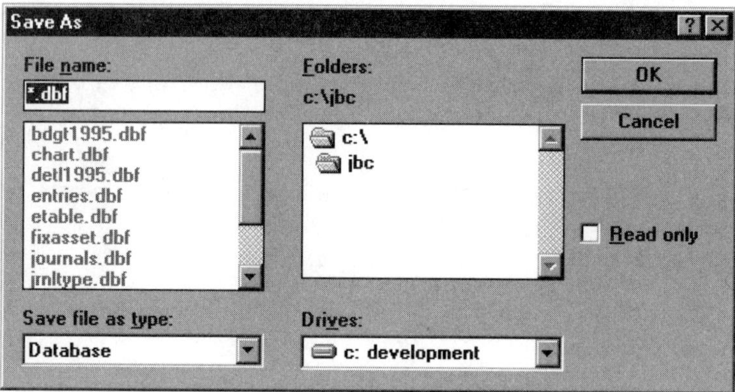

Figure 7.4 SaveDialog box —Windows 3.1 style.

Setting Dialog Properties

A number of properties can be set on the dialog object to control how it operates for the user. Many of these are similar to their counterparts in the **OpenDialog** object. In Visual Basic, the **OpenDialog** and **SaveDialog** common dialogs boxes share the same properties, so the values you set for one box are used by the other automatically.

Setting File Filters

The **Filter** property determines the file patterns available to the user to determine which files to display in the dialog box's list box. A file filter, sometimes called a file mask, is a file name that usually includes wildcard characters (*.DBF, for example). Only files that match the selected file filter are displayed in the dialog box's list box, and the selected file filter appears in the File Name edit box.

Default File Extension

The **DefaultExt** property specifies the extension that is added to the file name the user types in the File Name edit box if the user doesn't include a file-name extension in the file name. If the user specifies an extension for the file name, the value of the **DefaultExt** property is ignored. If the **DefaultExt** value is blank, no extension is added to the file name entered in the File Name edit box.

Specifying the Current Directory

The **InitialDir** (Delphi) / **InitDir** (Visual Basic) property determines the current directory when the dialog box first appears. After the dialog box appears, users can then use the directory tree to change to another directory. When specifying the initial directory, include the full path name. For example:

```
C:\WINDOWS\SYSTEM
```

If no initial directory or a directory that does not exist is specified, the directory that is current when the dialog box appears remains the current directory.

Changing the Title

The **Title** (Delphi) / **DialogTitle** (Visual Basic) property determines the text that appears in the dialog box's title bar.

Other Options

There are a large number of additional settings available. For instance, you can prompt when files will be overwritten and prevent the user from changing directories. By setting the proper options, the **SaveDialog** box can be used any time information needs to be written to the disk.

Calling the Dialog Box

After all of the properties are specified, control needs to be passed to the dialog box. In Delphi, this is done by using the **Execute** method of the particular dialog box. In Visual Basic, you need to call the **ShowSave()** method to invoke the file common dialog box. Once control is returned to the application from the dialog box, you can extract the various property values, most notably **filename** from the dialog box for use in the application.

FontDialog

The **FontDialog** component will create a common Windows Font selection dialog box that allows users to specify the name, size, and attribues of a font. When a user chooses a font from the dialog box, the font is assigned to the **Font** property of the object. You can than use this property value to set the font for a particular control or window.

Figure 7.5 shows the **FontDialog** component. The font dialog box looks very similar in both Windows 95 and Windows 3.1.

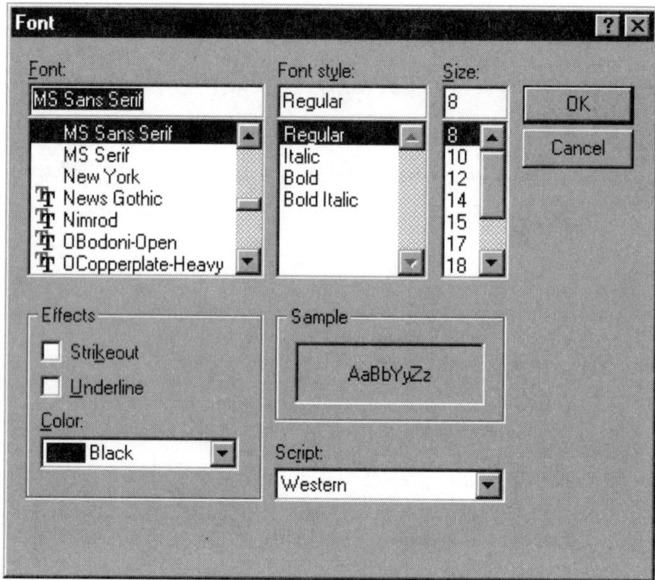

Figure 7.5 FontDialog box .

Setting Dialog Properties

There are a number of properties you can set on the font dialog object to determine which fonts the user may select and which type of font (i.e., screen or printer font) that the user may choose.

Device Property

The ***Device*** property (in Delphi) determines which device the returned font affects. These are the possible values:

Value	Meaning
fdScreen	Affects the screen
fdPrinter	Affects the printer
fdBoth	Affects both the screen and the printer

In Visual Basic, the affected device is controlled by the **flags** property. The following values (and possibly other options as well) can be specified in the Flags property. If you do not specify this value initially, Visual Basic will not be able to find any fonts.

Value	Meaning
cdlCFScreenFonts	Affects the screen
cdlCFPrinterFonts	Affects the printer
cdlCFBoth	Affects both the screen and the printer

Font Property

The **Font** property is the font that the **Font** dialog box returns when the user selects from the **Font** dialog box. Your application can then use this returned **Font** value for further processing.

You can also specify a default font before displaying the **Font** dialog box; the font name then appears selected in the **Font** combo box. Use the Object Inspector to specify a **Font** property, or assign a value to **Font** before using the **Execute** method (Delphi) or **ShowFont** method (Visual Basic) to display the dialog box.

Font Size Properties

The **MinFontSize** property (Delphi) / **Min** property (Visual Basic) determines the smallest font size available in the **Font** dialog box. Use the minimum size property when you want to limit the font sizes available to the user. To limit the font sizes available using Delphi, the **Options** property of the **Font** dialog box must also contain the value **fdLimitSize.** If **fdLimitSize** is False, setting the **MinFontSize** property has no affect on number of fonts available in the **Font** dialog box.

In Visual Basic, the **Flags** property must contain **cdlCFLimitSize** for font sizes to be limited.

The default value is zero, which means there is no minimum font size specified.

The **MaxFontSize** property (Delphi) / **Max** property (Visual Basic) determines the largest font size available in the **Font** dialog box. Use the maximum size property when you want to limit the font sizes available to the user. The default is that no maximum font size is specified.

Other Options

There are a large number of additional settings available. You can restrict the user to only certain type of fonts and you can control whether or not the special font effects (such as strikethru or underline) window appears in the dialog box. In Delphi, these options are stored in the **Options** property and in Visual Basic they are stored in the **Flags** property.

ColorDialog

The *ColorDialog* component creates a common Windows color selection dialog box that allows users to specify a color setting for some aspect of the program. When a user chooses a color from the dialog box, the color is assigned to the **Color** property of the object. This property value can be used to set the color for a particular control or window.

Figure 7.6 shows the **ColorDialog** component. This component looks the same in both Windows 95 and Windows 3.1.

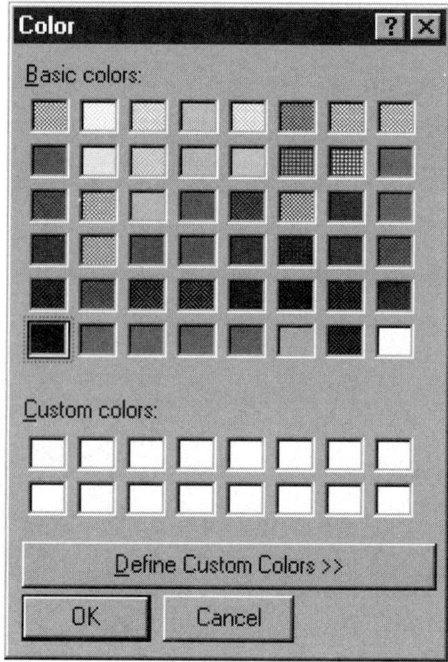

Figure 7.6 ColorDialog box.

Setting Dialog Properties

Only a few properties can be set on the color dialog object to determine what the user can do when selecting a color.

Options/Flags Property

These are the possible values that can be included in the **Options** property (in Delphi):

Value	Meaning
cdFullOpen	Show the custom coloring options when the dialog opens
cdPreventFullOpen	Disables the Create Custom Colors button in the **Color** dialog box, so the user cannot create their own custom colors.
cdShowHelp	Adds a Help button to the **Color** dialog box.

The default value is [ ], the empty set, meaning all of these values are False and none of the options are in effect.

In Visual Basic, the **Flags** property determines the possible options for the color selection dialog. The possible values are:

Value	Meaning
cdCClFullOpen	Show the custom coloring options when the dialog opens
cdlCCPreventFullOpen	Disables the Create Custom Colors button in the **Color** dia-log box, so the user cannot create their own custom colors.
cdlCCShowHelp	Adds a Help button to the **Color** dialog box.
cdlCCRGBInit	Sets the initial color to position the dialog at.

Using the Dialog box

After all of the properties are specified, control must be passed to the dialog box. In Delphi, this is done by using the **Execute** method of the particular dialog box. In Visual Basic, call the **ShowColor** method to invoke the color common dialog box. Once control is returned to the application from the color dialog box, you can extract the color property and set the form or some control to the selected color.

Listing 7.3 shows some Visual Basic code used to call the color dialog and set the form color to the user selection. Listing 7.4 shows the same procedure in Delphi.

Listing 7.3 Visual Basic using color dialog box.

```
Private Sub Form_Load()
    CommonDialog1.ShowColor
    Form1.BackColor = CommonDialog1.Color
End Sub
```

Listing 7.4 Delphi ColorDialog example.

```
procedure TForm1.FormClick(Sender: TObject);
begin
     if ColorDialog1.Execute then
        form1.color := colordialog1.color;
end;
```

PrintDialog

Whenever a report or memo needs to be printed, use the print dialog box to allow the user to select where to print to. The **PrintDialog** component will place a print dialog box on the screen and allow your user to select a printer destination, as well as number of copies, range, and collating sequence. When the user completes the dialog box, a number of properties will be useful for printing the output.

Figure 7.7 shows the print dialog box from Windows 95. Figure 7.8 shows the dialog box when running under Windows 3.1.

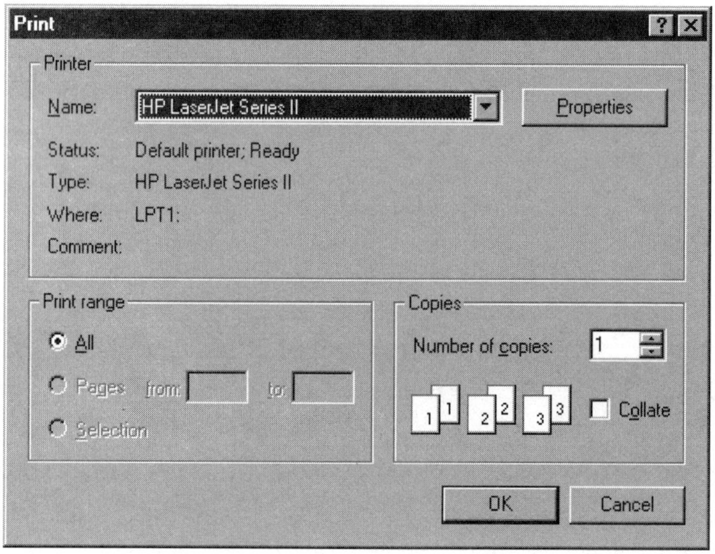

Figure 7.7 PrintDialog box—Windows 95.

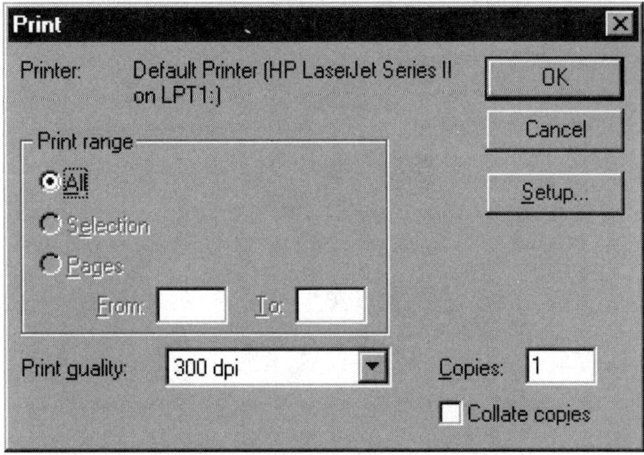

Figure 7.8 PrintDialog box—Windows 3.1.

Setting Dialog Properties

There are a number of properties that determine default values for printing.

Collate Property

The **Collate** (Delphi) property determines if the **Collate** check box is checked and, therefore, if collating is selected. Regardless of the initial setting of the **Collate** property, the user can always check or uncheck the **Collate** check box (and change the **Collate** property) to choose or not choose to collate the print job. The default setting is False. Collating is set using the Flags property discussed below in Visual Basic.

Copies Property

The **Copies** property determines the number of copies of the print job. The value of **Copies** is changed at design time, the value specified is the default value in the edit box control when the **Print** dialog box appears. The default value is zero.

MaxPage/Max Property

The **MaxPage** (in Delphi) / **Max** (in Visual Basic) property determines the greatest page number the user can use when specifying pages to print. If the user specifies a number greater than the value specified, a warning message appears and the user must enter a valid number or close the dialog box. The default value is zero.

NOTE

The user can specify pages numbers only if the **Options** property set includes the value **poPageNums**.

MinPage/Min Property

The **MinPage** (in Delphi) / **Min** (in Visual Basic) property determines the smallest page number the user can use when specifying pages to print. If the user specifies a number less than the value indicated, a warning message appears and the user must enter a valid number or close the dialog box. The default value is zero.

NOTE

The user can specify pages numbers only if the **Options** property set includes the value **poPageNums**.

Options / Flags Property

The **Options** (in Delphi) / **Flags** (in Visual Basic) property controls what options are available in the **Print** dialog box. For Delphi, the following values may be used in options.

Value	Meaning
poHelp	Causes a Help button to appear in the dialog box.
poPageNums	Enables the Pages radio button and the user can specify a range of pages.
poPrintToFile	A Print to File check box appears in the dialog box, giving the user the option to print to a file.
poSelection	The Selection radio button is enabled.
poWarning	A warning message appears when the user chooses **OK** and no printer is installed.
poDisablePrintToFile	The **Print to File** check box is dimmed when the dialog box appears.

For Visual Basic, the following values can be set in the flags property:

Value	Description
cdlPDAllPages	Sets the **All Pages** option button.
cdlPDCollate	Sets the **Collate** check box.
cdlPDDisablePrintToFile	Disables the **Print To File** check box.
cdlPDHidePrintToFile	Hides the **Print To File** check box.
cdlPDNoPageNums	Disables the **Pages** option button.
cdlPDNoSelection	Disables the **Selection** option button.
cdlPDNoWarning	Prevents a warning message from being displayed when there is no default printer.
cdlPDPageNums	Sets the Pages numbers option button.
cdlPDPrintSetup	Causes the system to display the Print Setup dialog box rather than the Print dialog box.
cdlPDPrintToFile	Sets the **Print To File** check box.
cdlPDSelection	Sets the state of the **Selection** option button.
cdlPDHelpButton	Causes the dialog box to display the Help button.

Using the Printer Dialog

Once you've set up the printer dialog options, call either the **Execute** method (Delphi) or the **ShowPrinter** method (Visual Basic). Upon its return, use the following properties to allow the application to decide what pages print.

FromPage / ToPage

These properties indicate the starting and ending page number the program should print.

PrinterSetupDialog

The **PrinterSetupDialog** component displays a **Printer Setup** dialog box in your application. Users can use the dialog box to setup their printer before printing a job. In Delphi, this is a separate component from the dialog palette. In Visual Basic, the **PrinterSetupDialog** box is called by setting the **cdlPDPrintSetup** flag to true on a common dialog object and then calling the **ShowPrinter** method. Figure 7.9 shows the printer setup dialog box from a Windows 95 application. Figure 7.10 shows the Windows 3.1 version.

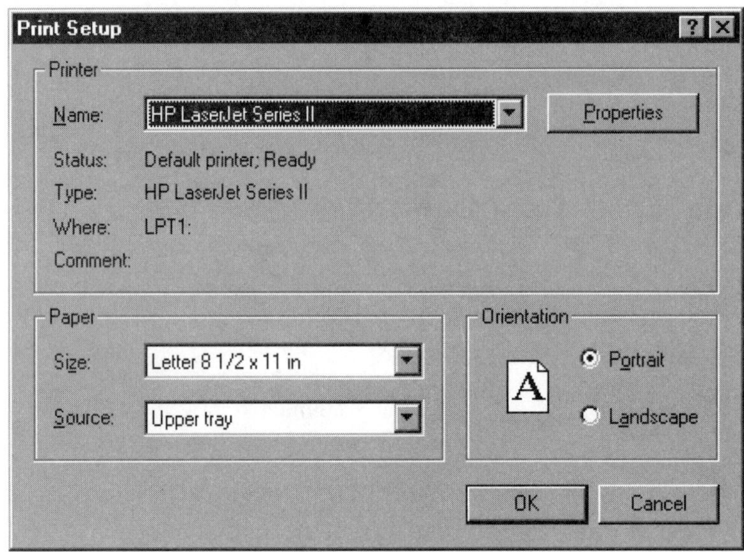

Figure 7.9 PrinterSetupDialog box—Windows 95.

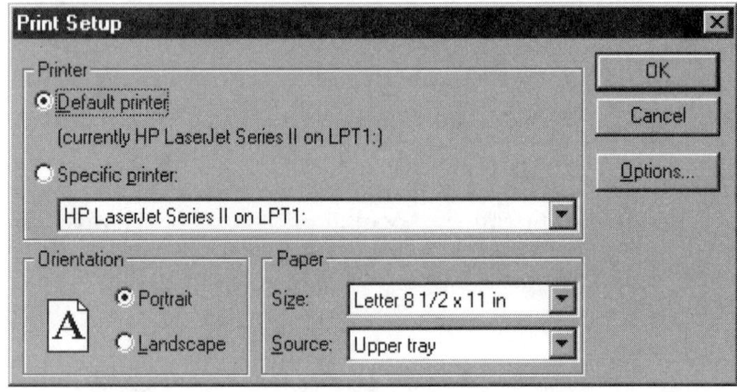

Figure 7.10 PrinterSetupDialog box—Windows 3.1.

Setting Dialog Properties

There is very little interaction needed with this dialog box. Merely call it and leave the details to Windows. Even though you don't need to do much programming with it, you should always make it available to your user either through a menu or a button.

FindDialog

The **findDialog** component is only found in Delphi (although it would be easy to visually design an form in Visual Basic if you so desired). It displays a box that allows the user to specify text to search for along with some search options. Figure 7.11 shows the FindDialog box from Delphi.

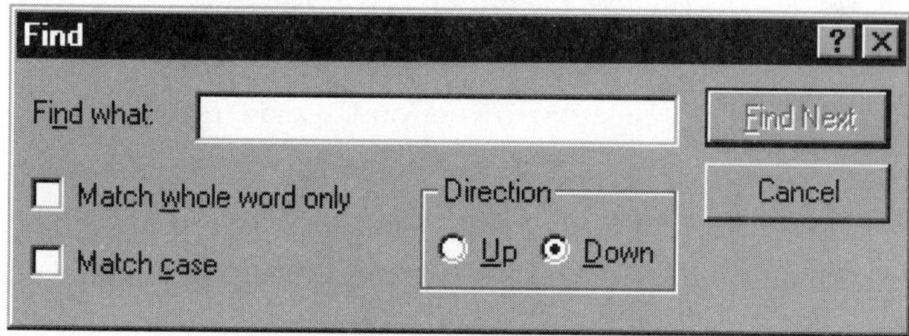

Figure 7.11 FindDialog box.

FindDialog Properties

Although there are only a few properties for the **findDialog** box, there are a large number of options you can set to control the process. With them, you should be able to set up the dialog to find just about anything.

FindText Property

The **FindText** property contains the string your application can search for if it uses the **Find** dialog box. You can specify a **FindText** value before the user displays the **Find** dialog box so that when it appears, the **FindText** value appears in the **Find What** edit box. The user can then either accept or change the **FindText** value before choosing the **Find Next** button in the dialog box.

Options Property

The **Options** property provides the control over how the dialog box operates. The following is a partial list of the settings available in **Options**.

Value	Meaning
frDisableMatchCase	Dims and disables the **Match Case** check box.
frDisableUpDown	Dims and disables the **Up** and **Down** buttons.
frDisableWholeWord	Dims and disables the match **Whole Word** check box
frDown	Sets the search direction to **Down**, which is the default.
frFindNext	This flag is set when the user chooses **Find Next**.
frHideMatchCase	Hides the **Match Case** check box
frHideWholeWord	Hides the **Match Whole Word** check box
frHideUpDown	Hides the **Direction Up** and **Down** buttons are visible.
frMatchCase	Enables and checks the **Match Case** check box
frShowHelp	A **Help** button appears in the dialog box
frWholeWord	Enables and checks the **Whole Word** check box

Using the Dialog Box

Once you've executed the dialog box, you should attempt to locate the value in the **FindText** property, subject to the values specified in the options.

ReplaceDialog

The **ReplaceDialog** box, also only in Delphi, presents the user with two strings. The first is the text to search for and the second is the text to replace it with. You should use this box any time you need to replace text. For example, you might want to replace all occurrences of a string within a text file, or you might want to update a text field in a DBF file. Both operations should use the replace dialog box, shown in Figure 7.12 to collect the information from the user.

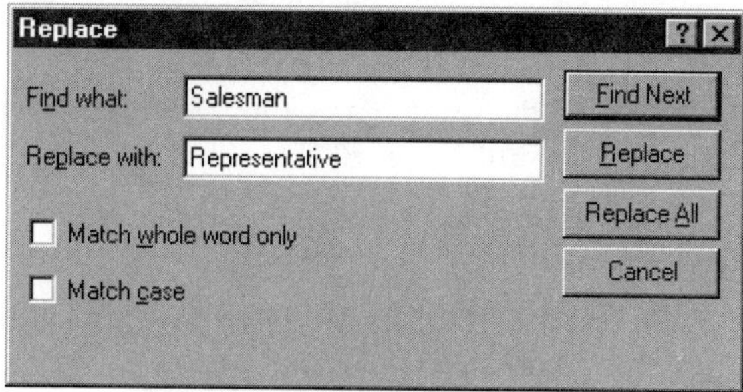

Figure 7.12 ReplaceDialog box.

The **ReplaceDialog** box is available only in Delphi; Visual Basic does not have a replace dialog in its common dialog object. There are only a few properties we need to work with, although there are a large number of options for customizing the box.

FindText Property

The **FindText** property contains the string your program displays in the **Find** dialog box. The user can then enter a new value for this property or can simply accept the text placed there. You would normally set a default value for the property and then called the methods. Subsequent calls would maintain the changed value that the user entered in the dialog box, which allows the user to do continual replacements without having to re-enter the text each time.

ReplaceText Property

The **ReplaceText** property contains the string your application should use to replace the string found in the **FindText** property when the specified text is found during a search. It will normally be updated after the user completes the dialog box.

Options Property

The **Options** property contains a number of options that control the box's appearance and the user's options. You can allow case insensitive matches, partial matches, and searches in either direction (up or down). The default option is to allow the user to specify case sensitivity and partial matches and to search down when looking for replacement text. In addition to the same options available to the find dialog box, the following options may also be returned after the user interacts with the dialog box.

Value	Meaning
frReplace	flag set by the system that indicates your application should replace the current occurrence of the FindText string with the ReplaceText string.
frReplaceAll	flag set by the system that indicates your application should replace all occurrences of the FindText string with the ReplaceText string.

Your program can then make the appropriate replacements based upon the option values and text settings in the **FindText** and **ReplaceText** properties.

Using Configuration Files

In DOS programming, we've all wrestled with where to store configuration about the application. Fortunately in Windows, there is a consistent spot for storing configuration information, .INI files. The .INI file is simply a text file that contains sections and entries. Your application can edit the .INI file or the user can edit it with a text editor.

In Windows 95, most Windows .INI files have been replaced by the repository. The repository is a single file that contains a collection of grouped entries, rather than multiple .INI files scattered on your hard drive. You can still use the .INI files for your own applications, however, rather than writing your changes directly into the repository.

Ini Files in Delphi

Delphi provides the **TIniFile** object, which permits your application to write and read an .INI file. An .INI file is an ASCII text file which is divided in sections and entries. Each section begins with the section name in brackets and is followed by any number of entries. Listing 7.5 shows a sample .INI file.

Listing 7.5 - Portion of Delphi.ini.

```
[Library]
ComponentLibrary=C:\DELPHI\BIN\SDE_BDE.DCL
SaveLibrarySource=0
```

```
MapFile=0
LinkBuffer=0
DebugInfo=0

[ReportSmith]
ExePath=C:\rptsmith

[Desktop]
SaveSymbols=0

[AutoSave]
EditorFiles=0
DesktopFile=1

[FormDesign]
DisplayGrid=1
SnapToGrid=1
GridSizeX=8
GridSizeY=8
```

Your application can retrieve all the string entries within a section of an .INI file by calling the **ReadSection** method; or it can retrieve a single Boolean, integer, or string value by calling the **ReadBool**, **ReadInteger**, or **ReadString** methods.

Creating a tIniFile Object

To create an ini file object, you need to specify the file name, as shown in the following syntax:

```
var
  IniFile: TIniFile;

begin
  IniFile := TIniFile.Create('BOOK.INI');

end;
```

Once you've opened the .INI file object, you can use a variety of methods to extract information from it.

ReadSection Method

The **ReadSection** method reads all the entries of a section of an .INI file into a string list object. The first parameter is the name of the section and the second is a special Delphi object called a string list. The string list object contains the contents of the indicated section.

Logical Entries

Logical (or Boolean) entries are values in the .INI file that contain either YES/NO, True/False, or 1/0. You can get the value of any logical value using the **ReadBool** method which takes three parameters, the section, the value, and a default logical setting. If the indicated entry does not exist, then the default value is returned, otherwise the entry is intepreted to determine whether it is true or false.

The **WriteBool** method allows writing an entry back to any section. Three parameters, the section, the entry text, and the value are required to write. If the entry exists within the section, its value will be updated. If the entry does not exists, it will be added to the section.

Numeric Entries

Numeric entries are values in the INI file that contain some numeric value. The value of any numeric entry can be obtained using the **ReadInteger** method which takes three parameters, the section, the value, and a default numeric setting. If the indicated entry does not exist, then the default value is returned, otherwise the integer value of the entry is returned.

The **WriteInteger** method allows writing an entry back to any section. You need three parameters, the section, the entry text, and the value to write. If the entry exists within the section, its value will be updated. If the entry does not exist, it will be added to the section.

Character Entries

String entries are values in the .INI file that contain character values. You can get the value of any such entry using the **ReadString** method which takes three parameters, the section, the value, and a default value. If the indicated entry does not exist, then the default value is returned, otherwise the string value of the entry is returned.

The **WriteString** method allows writing an entry back to any section. You need three parameters, the section, the entry text, and the value to write. If the entry exists within the section, its value will be updated. If the entry does not exist, it will be added to the section.

EraseSection Method

To erase an entire section of an .INI file, use the **EraseSection** method. This method takes the section you want to erase as a parameter and will remove all entries from that section.

Freeing the Object

Any time you create your own object in Delphi (using the **Create** method), it is necessary to free the object and its memory when you are done with it. This is done by simply calling the **free** method.

The Mouse Pointer

In DOS programming, the mouse is more often thought of as a luxury rather than an essential navigation tool. Yet in Windows, the mouse is an integral part of the design and the users are comfortable with it. The mouse pointer provides a visual cue to the user about what actions are allowed in the control or on the form.

Design-time Mouse Changes

When you are designing forms, you can have the mouse shape change for each control on the form. The **Cursor** property (Delphi) / **MousePointer** property (Visual Basic) specifies the image used when the mouse passes into the region covered by the control. These are the possible images:

Delphi	Visual Basic	Image
crDefault	0=Default	Default, arrow shaped cursor
crArrow	1=Arrow	Another arrow shaped cursor
crCross	2=Cross	A cross shaped cursor
crIBeam	3=I-Beam	Usually used during text entry
crSize	5=Size	Sizing cursor to change a window's size
crSizeNESW	6=Size NE SW	Double-sided arrow pointing NE and SW
crSizeNS	7=Size NS	Double sided arrow pointing North/South
crSizeNWSE	8=Size NW SE	Double sided arrow pointing NW and SE
crSizeWE	9=Size WE	Double sided arrow pointing West/East
crUpArrow	10=Up arrow	Arrow point straight up
crHourglass	11=Hourglass	Hour-glass for time-consuming tasks
crNoDrop	12=No Drop	Cursor indicating drag & drop won't work

Run-time Mouse Pointer Changes

At certain times during your program, you should inform the user of allowed or disallowed options. The mouse pointer can be used to provide visual cues which most Windows users will recognize. For example, when the mouse pointer is the hourglass symbol, it is time for a brief snack or coffee break.

Summary

Windows programming is different from DOS. Just porting your DOS program into Windows is not enough for most users. Your program should have the same look and feel as other Windows programs. Using the common dialogs, .INI files, and bitmaps, are all part of the standard tools in Windows to achieve that consistency. Take the time to explore and use them when you are writing Windows programs. Look at existing programs and decide what you like best and mimic it. While you can be very creative in what your program does, consistency is important in the user interface portion.

CHAPTER 8:

THROWING AWAY THE MENU

One of the first questions that must be answered when designing any system is, "What is the system going to do?" That high-level objective is taken and broken down into a series of meaningful, related tasks. DOS programmers, typically rely upon menu structures to control how the user navigates among these tasks.

Windows programming does not want to control the user's navigation, but rather wants the user to reign free over the program. While a DOS menu restricts the user into a narrow set of choices, a Windows menu is generally secondary to the program, provides an alternate way of navigating a screen, and is not necessary to the application. Therefore, we should not begin with the menu and in some cases, might not even need one at all.

Updating Customers—A DOS Program

Let's examine a DOS program written in Xbase that allows the user to add/edit/delete accounts from the ledger. In addition, the program can search for a particular account by either number or title and can print the financial statements. In Chapter 1, a menu structure was created that would allow the user to navigate to this ledger edit screen. Figure 8.1 illustrates a sample screen used to edit the general ledger.

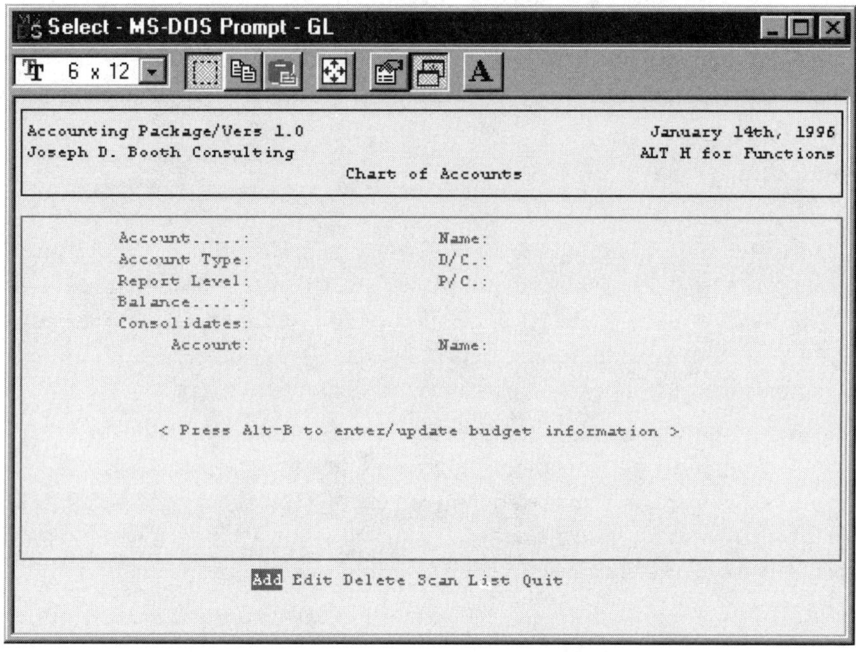

Figure 8.1 DOS-based general ledger editing screen.

This program not only relies on the menu to the ledger, but also in choosing the option (the horizontal menu of choices at the bottom). If print is selected, another pop-up menu appears which allows the user to select the desired financial statement and the print destination.

While looking at it in this kind of negative view, it makes overuse of menus seem problematic; but for many users, menus are a comforting, easy tool to use that doesn't tax their memories. Keep the your audience in mind when designing Windows programs. Programs can easily be designed in Windows without using a menu, but make sure the users will be comfortable with that approach.

Updating Accounts—A Windows Version

Let's look at the same program for updating accounts, but from a Windows programming perspective. Begin with a blank form and add the components and code that allow the user to perform the same functionality as the DOS counterpart program.

Our First Version

The initial design looks like Figure 8.2, which is menu based just like the DOS version.

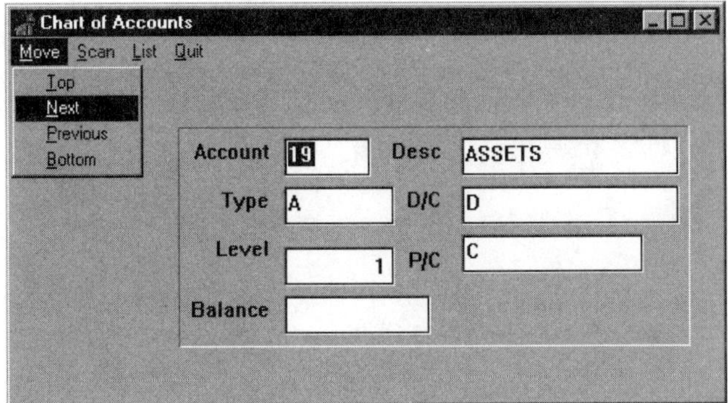

Figure 8.2 Menu driven Windows program.

While this program looks similar to the DOS counterpart and provides similar functionality, even a new Windows user will probably find it awkward. The program is not structured in the same way they are used to doing things in Windows.

Try Again

Let's design the same functionality, however, this time, without the menu. A method to navigate the chart of accounts, to search, and to produce financial reports must be provided. The ability to leave the screen is also required. Figure 8.3 shows the result of replacing the menu with a variety of controls.

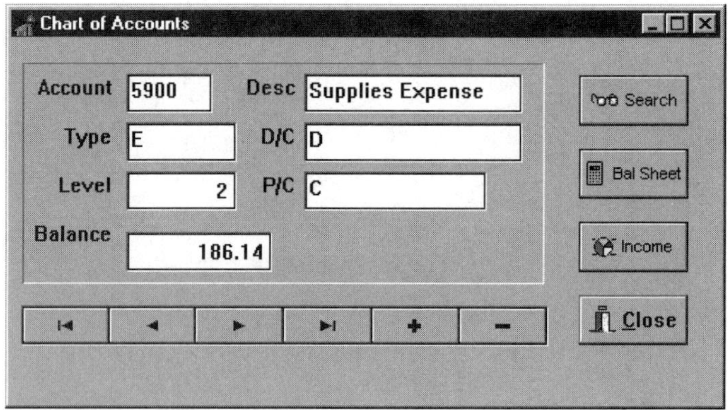

Figure 8.3 Windows-based general ledger editing screen.

Although this simple window does not have a menu to control it, it still contains all of the functionality of the DOS counterpart. Navigating through the database is controlled with the arrows keys below the screen—similar to a VCR's remote control. Searching and reporting are available at the click of a button. Best of all, it looks and feels much more like a Windows program than the first version.

Don't Totally Give Up the Menu

Even though for this application is not using a menu, we could easily add one to make the program easier to use. The most important factor is that the menu is not a restriction tool, but rather is a supplemental navigation method. With that in mind, put the menu back in the program. The menu will be on one line at the top of the screen, however, it can be easily accessed if the user wants it. Figure 8.4 shows the final screen, combining both the menu and the controls.

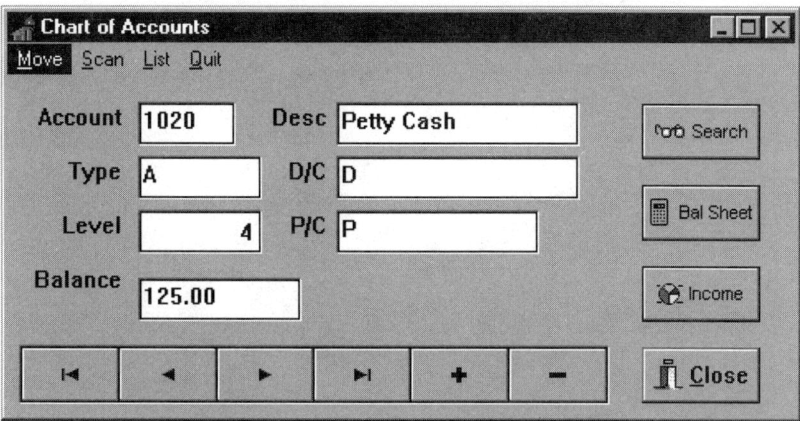

Figure 8.4 Final chart of accounts program.

Although this illustrates how the menu and controls can be combined, you may want to go one step further. The menu prompt text should agree with the text on the buttons. After all, if Scan on the menu performs the same functionality as the **Search** button, the same word should be used to describe it.

Going Even Further

Many times, an application will rely solely on the images on the buttons, particularly when there are a large number of them. For example, Figure 8.5 shows the toolbar from Lotus' Ami-Pro word processor. While some of the buttons are obvious, some are not so readily apparent.

Figure 8.5 Ami-Pro's toolbar.

To assist users in trying to interpret these buttons, Windows provides a hint or fly-by help. Both Visual Basic and Delphi provide support for hints, allowing you to save a little message and cause it to appear whenever the cursor moves over a particular item. In Figure 8.6, a hint has been added to the arrows on the navigation bar.

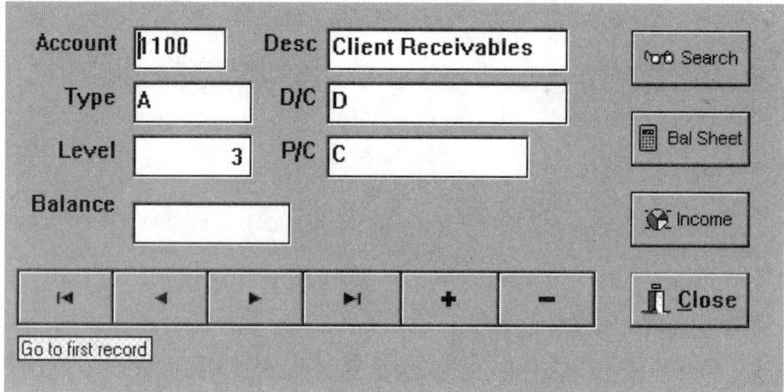

Figure 8.6 Hint on the navigation bar.

While the menu can make the screen easier to use, particular for a DOS user who has grown accustomed to menus, it is certainly not a required part of the screen. Try to provide your users with multiple methods of accomplishing the needed tasks, resulting in different users being able to work with the system easily.

A Call Tracking Program

Let's look at a simple example program where a menu shouldn't be used. Imagine you are designing a simple program to keep track of phones calls received and made. The program should be available all the time and only activated when the user receives or makes a phone call. All other times, the program sits quietly on the task bar, waiting to be activated.

Designing the System

The first part of the system is to determine what exactly the call tracking program must do. There are three basic tasks:

A. Record incoming/outgoing calls

B. Search for calls by a wide variety of criteria

C. Print various call reports

A DOS-based system would contain a simple menu system with three options and some sub-menus. However, one requirement is that the program should be minimized at most times and the user should be able to call it and start recording the phone call as soon as he picks up the phone.

Screen Design

The screen should be simple and easy to fill out. The basic information that needs to be collected and stored is the date and time of the call, the person's name and phone number, and a brief note as to the subject of the call. For good measure, we can also include the status of the phone call, i.e., follow-up, resolved, etc.

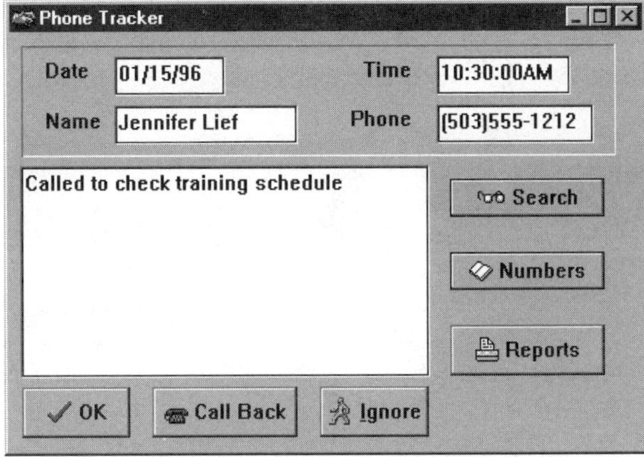

Figure 8.7 Our screen design.

When the program is run, the system starts at the date and time of a new record. The user simply accepts the default date and time and tabs twice to enter the person's name and number. Upon completion, the program is minimized and sits quietly waiting for the next phone call.

The user may also click on the search or number buttons to look for text with notes or to find phone numbers. Clicking on reports will present a menu of the standard reports the system can produce.

This simple application is designed to perform familiar process. It is simple to use, but could quite easily be improved. The missing piece is that while this application is simple and easy to use, it totally ignores an object that the user is familiar with—the "WHILE-U-WERE-OUT" message slip. These are completed all the time and everyone knows how to do it. We should take advantage of that knowledge when designing our programs.

Another Variation

Let's redesign our simple application, only this time mimicking the familiar. Figure 8.8 shows the sample functionality as the program we designed above, but the user will most likely know how to use it immediately.

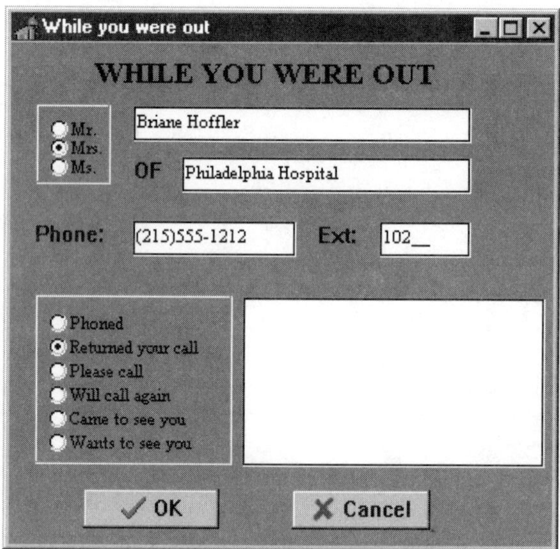

Figure 8.8 A different version of the phone program.

Don't miss opportunities to model systems in a way that is most familiar to the user. With the tremendous graphical capabilities of Windows, plan to write screens that look like the physical objects of the system's users already know how to use. DOS programmers can't do this as easily and the menu system has come to be an alternative approach. Windows programmers, however, should take advantage of everything Windows has to offer.

Object-Based Design

In Chapter 3, we discussed CUA concepts. One of those concepts is that CUA is based upon the users ability to manipulate objects. Most objects in the real world, however, do not come with menus attached to them. The following are some examples of real world objects being modeled by Windows programming, without using a menu structure.

Lotus Organizer

A good example a Windows program that does not need a menu—although it does provide one—is the Lotus Organizer program. Figure 8.9 shows the main organizer screen.

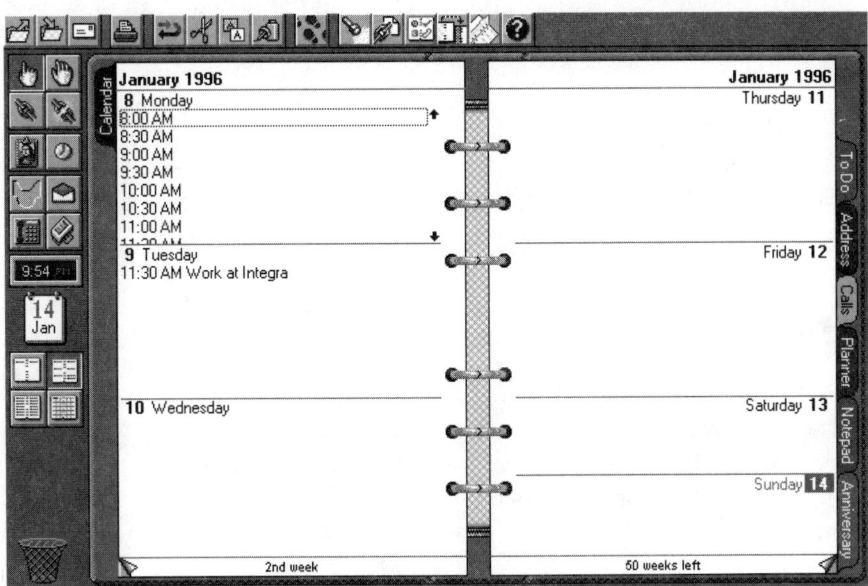

Figure 8.9 Lotus Organizer screen.

This program is very simple and intuitive to use. A DOS program based on a menu structure attempting to perform the same functionality would be very awkward to use. Lotus Organizer's simple, visual design makes it easy to use, without relying on a menu.

Packard Bell's CD Player

A Packard Bell computer provides a handy program for playing music CDs. Figure 8.10 shows the CD player and volume control program under Windows 95.

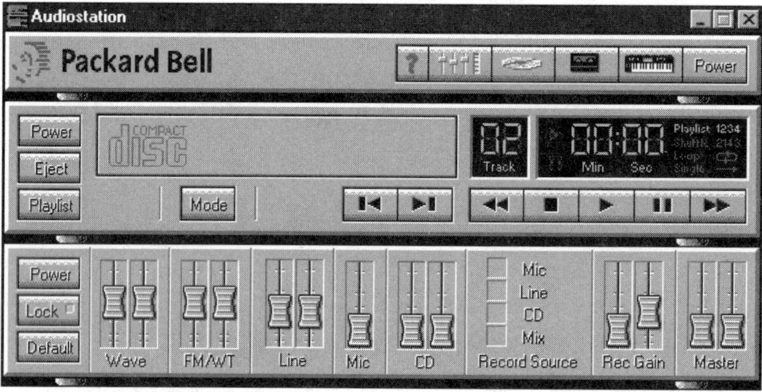

Figure 8.10 CD player / volume control.

Both of these examples are user friendly because the user intuitively knows how to work the object being represented. Take advantage of what you user already knows to make your software easier and more approachable. Design your screens to provide the user with access to objects, not menus.

Summary

The menu is a handy tool in a DOS program and provides the programmer with an easy way to organize related tasks. Many programmers tend to use menus as outliners to keep track of what needs to be done. Windows programming can be a little intimidating at first, particularly when it seems one of your organizational tools is gone. However, feel free to keep the menu outline if it helps to organize your code easier; just don't force your user to rely on it.

CHAPTER 9:
BEHIND THE SCENES

The first chapters explored many of the visual tools that Delphi and Visual Basic offer for program development. Programs can be easily and quickly designed, and complete applications can be assembled with very little programming. Yet, behind the scenes is a programming language which provides those other little tasks that need to be accomplished, but aren't quite as glamorous as their visual counterparts. In this chapter, we will explore the language, focusing on some of the more common Xbase tasks that aren't visual in nature. This should provide insight to the languages behind the tools.

Object Pascal and Basic

Delphi's core language is called Object Pascal, which makes sense because Borland's first product was Turbo Pascal 1.0. Object Pascal is a complete, object-oriented version of Pascal. Some people complain that Pascal is an educational language rather than a commercial language like C or COBOL, and therefore should be avoided. Of course, some people insist that Xbase is not a true language. However you look at it, Object Pascal is an elegant implementation of a solid language.

Visual Basic, as the name implies, is based upon the BASIC language. BASIC stands for Beginners All-Purpose Symbolic Instruction Code. Despite a name that implies it is for beginners, Microsoft's implementation of BASIC in Visual Basic contains a lot of power. It is the same BASIC used to provide macro programming capability in Excel and Microsoft Word. True to its name, BASIC is a simple language to learn, yet Visual Basic provides quite a bit of capability while still retaining a good degree of ease of use.

Whichever language you work in, one thing to keep in mind is that they are not Xbase languages. Certain things in Xbase have no counterpart in either language and vice-versa. You'll probably find the languages a bit more picky than the Xbase language you've worked with in the past, particularly Object Pascal's requirement that all variables be declared and typed.

Data Types

In Xbase, a variable data type is determined by what you place in it. There is nothing wrong (at least within the syntax of Xbase) with the following lines of code:

```
paid_on   = date()
if paid_amt < bal_due
    paid_on = "STILL OPEN"
endif
? paid_on
```

This process is referred to as loose typing, which simply means that the variable's data type is determined and run-time and can change without any special conversion routines. This makes good sense in a language that was designed to be an interpreter-based, data-query language. Most compilers, however, require that a type be declared for a variable. This means that a value cannot be assigned to that variable unless it is of that specific type. This allows the compiler to prepare the memory to work with the variables in advance, rather than at run-time.

Object Pascal's Data Types

Delphi's language offers a variety of data types which can be loosely grouped into the following four categories:

Simple Types

The simple data types consist of two subtypes, real numbers and ordinal data types. Real numbers are numeric values that are not restricted to integer values, but can include decimal places. In Xbase, the Float data type supported in FoxPro and dBASE IV+ are the closest equivalent data types. Clipper 5.3a has also added support for the float data type.

While Xbase provides a single float type for non-integer numerics, Object Pascal provides five different variations of real numbers. The primary difference among them is the range of values you can store in them. As a general rule, use the smallest data type that will support your usage of the number. Table 9.1 shows Delphi's data types for real numbers.

Table 9.1 Delphi Real Number Data Types

Type	Range	Digits	Bytes
Real	2.9 * 10-39 .. 1.7 * 1038	11-12	6
Single	1.5 * 10-45 .. 3.4 * 1038	7-8	4
Double	5.0 * 10-324 .. 1.7 * 10308	15-16	8
Extended	3.4 * 10-4932 .. 1.1 * 104932	19-20	10
Comp	-263+1 .. 263-1	19-20	8

Ordinal data types in Object Pascal are a data type that contains a finite number of possible values. In Xbase programming, we tend not to view our data types as ordinal, since the size of the data can vary. However, a character field in a DBF file with a length of one is an ordinal data type, because the range of possible values is finite, between 0 and 255. Table 9.2 lists the some of the ordinal data types.

Table 9.2 Object Pascal's Ordinal Types

Type	Range	Xbase function
ShortInt	-128..127	
SmallInt	-32768..32767	Bin2I() and I2Bin()
LongInt	-214748368..214647367	
Byte	0..255	
Word	0..65535	Bin2W() and L2Bin()
Boolean	true (1) .. false(0)	Xbase's logical data type
Char	ASCII characters	Asc() and Chr()

In addition to the predefined ordinal data types, Object Pascal allows an enumerated list data type. This is similar to fixed size array in Xbase. For example, the following code in Xbase:

```
aWeekdays     = array(5)
aWeekdays[1]  = "Monday"
aWeekdays[2]  = "Tuesday"
aWeekdays[3]  = "Wednesday"
aWeekdays[4]  = "Thursday"
aWeekdays[5]  = "Friday"
```

could be represented as an enumerated list in Object Pascal, as shown below:

```
type
 aWeekdays = ( Monday,Tuesday,Wednesday,Thursday,Friday)
```

Enumerated types allow you to write code using the type values, i.e., Monday, Friday, rather than numeric codes. After all, which is easier to read?

```
if nDayCode = 4
 then ShipNextDay()
elseif nDayCode = 5
 then FaxIt()
else
 then ShipTwoDay()
```

```
if nDayCode = Thursday
then ShipNextDay()
  elseif nDayCode = Friday
then FaxIt()
else
then ShipTwoDay()
```

In addition to readability, Object Pascal provides a number of functions, such as determining the current position in the list, the next element, and so on. These functions work on all ordinal types, not just the enumerated list.

String Types

String types are the same as Xbase character types, except that they are limited to a maximum of 255 characters. A smaller string type can be created by reducing the maximum number of characters. The default is the Delphi string maximum of 255 characters.

A string type in Delphi actual acts like an array, where you can access individual characters in the string by using an index to their position. The first character in the string is at position 1, the second character at position 2, and so on. The length of the string is stored in the 0 element as a byte.

Delphi also has a data type known as a PCHAR. This data type is basically a pointer to a section in memory where a variable length string, up to 64K can be stored.

Xbase strings operate more similar to PCHAR, with variable lengths of up to 64K, than with strings, which wreaks a bit of havoc on memory. In a compiled environment, the use of strings rather than PCHAR is much more efficient. However, in the interpretive environment that Xbase grew from, asking the user to pre-guess the string's size is not user-friendly.

Structured Types

Object Pascal supports structured data types, which are data types that hold more than one occurrence of each data element. For example, Xbase's arrays would be classified as a structured data type in Object Pascal. Similar to Xbase arrays, structured types can manipulate individual items or the entire structure, much like using array[index] versus the **aSort** function. However, Object Pascal has some additional structured types beyond the array. Delphi's structured types include:

```
array types
object types
record types
set types
```

Array Types

Arrays are one dimensional or multidimensional containers that hold multiple variables of the same data type. This is similar to Xbase arrays. although Xbase provides support for different data types among array elements. Array elements are referenced by specifying the array name and an index number in brackets.

One of the handy features of arrays is that the elements themselves can be arrays, allowing you to create multidimensional arrays. You can then specify the array element using two or more indexes. The arrays must be uniform in size. This is primarily because the compiler needs to set aside static memory space at the loading of a module, rather than dynamically allocate space at run-time.

Object Types

An object type is a structure consisting of a fixed number of components. The components are any mixture of the following types:

fields
methods
properties

Object types are a large part of Object Pascal, as most components are objects. In addition to the built in objects, you can create your own object classes. If you are familiar with the object classes in the various Xbase languages, you will probably feel comfortable with Object Pascal's object type. There are a large number of methods and special coding concerns when dealing with objects, although proper use of objects can create a much easier system to design and maintain.

Record Types

A record type is similar to the DBF field layout, except that it is in memory as a variable. The record can consist of any number of fields, subject to some sizing constraints. Each field can be a different data type.

A record type can have two parts, a fixed part which is like the fields in a DBF file, and a variant part which allows different field layouts to occupy the same space in memory. Usually a flag in the fixed part indicates which variant to use to interpret the memory.

The whole record or each field individually can be accessed. To access an individual field, type the record name, a period, and the field identifier. For example, a record type called invoice might have a po_num field and a sales_tax amount, presumably with some additional fields. To access the entire record, refer to the INVOICE variable. To access the po_num field, use the syntax INVOICE.PO_NUM, which looks very much like an accepted way to access fields with FoxPro, although the -> operator is more common in Xbase.

Set Types

A set type is a collection of data made up of the same ordinal type. A set variable may hold none or all the values of the set. Every set type can hold the value [ ], which is called the empty set. Set types are useful when you need to have multiple options or settings grouped within a variable. Operators allow joining sets and testing if items are included in the set or not.

Additional Types

There are a number of additional data types in Object Pascal, such as pointers and procedural types, which provide a good deal of power to the language. To give you an example of the power of the language, the Delphi IDE was written mostly in Delphi. Although we won't go into technical details about Object Pascal many benefits, if you work with Delphi, the underlying core language will provide you access to just about anything you need to accomplish.

Visual Basic's Data Types

Visual Basic's language offers a variety of data types which can be loosely grouped into the following five categories, which more closely resemble Xbase data types.

Most data types are distinguish by the final character in the variable name, i.e., $ on the end of a variable indicates a string variable.

Numeric Types

The numeric types can be grouped into two groups, one group for real numbers and a second group for integers. The real number data types are single, double, and currency. The primary difference between them is the size of the number. The integer data types are byte, integer, and long, again distinguished by their size.

Single

Single (single-precision floating-point) variables are stored as 4-byte floating-point numbers, ranging in value from -3.402823E38 to -1.401298E-45 for negative values and from 1.401298E-45 to 3.402823E38 for positive values. You can declare a single data type using the exclamation point (!) on the end of the variable name, for example MonthSalary! = 3304.

Double

Double (double-precision floating-point) variables are stored as 8-byte floating-point numbers ranging from -1.79769313486232E308 to -4.94065645841247E-324 for negative values and from 4.94065645841247E-324 to 1.79769313486232E308 for positive values. The type-declaration character for the double data type is the pound sign (#), i.e. Yearly Quota # = 6500000.

Currency

Currency variables are stored as 8-byte numbers in an integer format multiplied by 10,000 to give a fixed-point number with 15 digits to the left of the decimal point and 4 digits to the right. This provides a range of -922,337,203,685,477.5808 to 922,337,203,685,477.5807. The type-declaration character for currency is @, SalesPrice@ = 600000.

Byte

Byte variables are stored as single, unsigned, 8-bit (1-byte) ranging in value from 0 to 255. This is the smallest numeric integer storage in Visual Basic. Byte variables are good for looping variables and other variables of short duration with a small range of values. There is no type declaration character for byte integers.

Integer

Integer variables are stored as 16-bit (2-byte) numbers ranging in value from -32,768 to 32,767. The type-declaration character for the integer data type is %, i.e. ctr% = 10.

Long

The long integer is similar to the integer data type, but twice as big. Long variables are stored as signed 32-bit (4-byte) numbers ranging in value from -2,147,483,648 to 2,147,483,647. The type-declaration character for the long data type is &, opCode& = 02.

String Types

There are two kinds of string variables available in Visual Basic. Variable-length strings, which can contain up to approximately 2 billion characters (or 64K characters for Microsoft Windows version 3.1 and earlier). This is the string type you are probably most familiar with from Xbase, although very few Xbase products allow strings larger than 64K (which is primarily a restriction based upon the DOS addressing scheme).

Fixed-length strings, which can contain 1 to approximately 64K characters, are very similar to Object Pascal's strings. The only difference between these and variable length strings is that you specify the maximum string size as the variable is created. Although this makes thing easier for the compiler, it is not part of the intuitive Xbase language design.

The type-declaration character for String is $. The codes for String characters range from 0 to 255. The first 128 characters (0–127) of the character set correspond to the letters and symbols on a standard U.S. keyboard from the ASCII character set. The second 128 characters (128–255) represent special characters, such as letters in international alphabets, accents, currency symbols, and fractions.

Boolean Types

Boolean variables are stored as 16-bit (2-byte) numbers, but they can only be True or False. Boolean variables display as either True / #TRUE# or False/ #FALSE#, depending upon the command used to display them. Use the keywords True and False to assign one of the two states to Boolean variables.

Date Types

Date variables are stored as IEEE 64-bit (8-byte) floating-point numbers that represent dates ranging from 1 January 100 to 31 December 9999 and times from 0:00:00 to

23:59:59. Any recognizable literal date values can be assigned to Date variables. Literal dates must be enclosed within number sign characters (#), for example, #January 1, 1993# or #1 Jan 93#.

Date variables display dates according to the short date format recognized by your computer. Times display according to the time format (either 12- or 24-hour) recognized by your computer.

Variant Data Type

The Variant data type is the type that all variables become if not explicitly declared as some other type. There is no type-declaration character for variant data. Like Xbase, the variant type can contain any kind of data except user-defined types and fixed length strings. A Variant can also contain the special values Empty, Error, Nothing, and Null.

The value Empty denotes a Variant variable that hasn't been initialized (assigned an initial value). A Variant containing Empty is 0 if it is used in a numeric context and a zero-length string (“”) if it is used in a string context.

Basic Programming Constructs

While we don't want to write a primer on either language, it is useful to look at some of the Xbase programming constructs and see their counterparts in Delphi and Visual Basic. You'll be comforted to know that all the looping and conditionals in Xbase can be easily done in Delphi and VB.

Conditionals

Conditional statements are a major part of any programming language, Visual Basic and Delphi are no exception. The two key conditional statements from Xbase, the ***if..else..endif*** and ***do case...endcase*** have counterparts in VB and Delphi, with slight variations in syntax.

if ... else ... endif

Both Visual Basic and Delphi have the ***if..else..then*** construct which provides the same function as Xbase's ***if ...else...endif***. In Object Pascal, the syntax is:

```
if  <condition> then
   <statement>
else
   <statement>  ;
```

The condition must evaluate to a logical value. If it is true, then the statement after the then clause is performed. If the condition is false, the statement after the else (if the else clause is used) is performed. Each statement (after the then and the else clauses) can only be one command or function call. However, you can imbed multiple statements in a ***begin.. end*** block if you want to have more than one statement executed. For example:

```
if <condition> then
  begin
    <statement>;
    <statement>;
  end;
```

If you work in Delphi, be sure to understand how statements operate. It is easy to forget the single statement after the then rule, which can cause some unexpected behaviors. In Visual Basic, the syntax is similar to Object Pascal, except that multiple statements can be performed without any special blocking. The syntax is:

```
IF <condition > THEN <statements> [ELSE statements ]
```

or, alternatively

```
IF <condition> THEN
 [statements]
[ELSEIF <condition> THEN
 [statements] . . .
[ELSE
 [statements]
END IF
```

The condition is some Visual Basic expression that evaluates to a logical true/false results. If the condition is true, the statements following the appropriate THEN clause will be performed. If no conditions are true, the statements following the ELSE clause, if present, will be executed.

do case... endcase

Both Visual Basic and Delphi have a case construct to handle code in which multiple conditions need to be tested. In Object Pascal, the syntax is:

```
case <variable> of
   <first value to compare>  :  <statement to execute if match> ;
   <second value to compare> :  <statement to execute if match> ;
   < addition comparisons>   : < additional statements> ;
else
   < otherwise statement > ;
end;
```

In the case statement, the variable is often a numeric data type. The comparison values are listed one line at a time, following by a colon. If the variable matches any of the values in the comparison list, the statement to the right of the colon will be performed. If the entire list is processed without a match, then the ELSE statement, if one is present, will be executed. For example, consider the following Object Pascal code to determine how to ship.

```
case nDayCode of
 Thursday   :  ShipNextDay ;
 Friday     :  FaxIt ;
else
 ShipTwoDay;
end;
```

In Visual Basic, multiple conditions can be tested using the **SELECT CASE** statement. Its syntax is:

```
SELECT CASE  <variable>
[CASE <expressions>
 [statements] . . .
[CASE ELSE
 [statements]
END SELECT
```

The **<variable>** is the name of the variable to be test in each of the **CASE** clauses. The expressions are possible values for the variable. If the variable meets any of the expressions, then the appropriate statements are executed. If no expressions meet the value of the variable, then the **CASE ELSE** statements are performed. For example:

```
Weight  = 30                              ' Initialize variable.
SELECT CASE Weight                        ' Evaluate Weight
CASE 1 TO 25                              ' Between 1 and 25.
 Print "Ship UPS Ground"
CASE 26 TO 50                             ' Between 26 and 50 pounds
 Print "Ship Federal Express"
CASE IS > 50
 Print "Ship Airbourne Express"
CASE ELSE
 Print "Invalid weight was specified"
END SELECT
```

Looping Constructs

Xbase provides two basic looping constructs, the **for... next** loop and the **do while** loop. Delphi and Visual Basic also support looping constructs. In Object Pascal, there are three looping constructs; **for..to, while... do, repeat...until**

for...to loop

The ***for*** statement causes the statement after the ***do*** clause to be executed once for each value between the initial and final value, inclusive. Its syntax is:

```
for <var>  := <nStart> to|downto <nEnd>  do <statement> ;
```

The **<var>** is the control variable, which should be a simple numeric data type (probably an integer, although that is not a requirement). **<nStart>** is the initial starting value for the variable and **<nEnd>** is the ending variable. If you use the **TO** keyword, the nEnd should be higher than nStart and counting will be ascending. The **DOWNTO** keyword expects high to low and counts descending.

If you need to execute multiple statements, be sure to wrap them in a **BEGIN..END** pair, since the do clause expects a single statement after it.

while ... do

A ***while*** statement controls the repeated execution of a singular or compound statement. The statement after the ***do*** clause executes as long as the Boolean expression is True. The expression is evaluated before the statement is executed, so if the expression is False at the beginning, the statement is not executed. The syntax is:

```
WHILE <condition>         DO <statement> ;
```

If you need to execute multiple statements, be sure to wrap them in a **BEGIN..END** pair, since the **do** clause expects a single statement after it.

repeat ...until

The statements between **repeat** and **until** are executed in sequence while the Boolean expression in the until statement evaluates to True. Using this loop ensures that the sequence is executed at least once because the Boolean expression is evaluated after the execution of each sequence. Its syntax is:

```
repeat
 <statements> ;
 <more statements>;
until <condition> ;
```

Visual Basic Looping

Visual Basic also has three looping constructs you can use for repeating blocks of code. These are: **do...loop, for...next,** and **while...wend**

do...loop

This construct repeats a group of statements while a condition is True or until a condition becomes True. Its syntax is: .

```
DO [{WHILE | UNTIL} <condition> ]
 [statements]
 [EXIT DO]
 [statements]
LOOP
```

Or, you can use this equally valid syntax:

```
DO
 [statements]
 [EXIT DO]
 [statements]
LOOP [{WHILE | UNTIL} <condition> ]
```

The first sequence is similar to the while...do in Object Pascal, in that the series of statements are only executed after the condition is tested, and possibly not at all. The second syntax force the statements to be executed at least once, since the condition is tested afterwards. The WHILE clause causes the program to keep looping as long as the condition is true, and the UNTIL clause keeps looping until the condition becomes True.

for...next

The **for...next** loop repeats a series of statements a specified number of times. Its syntax is:

```
FOR <counter> = <start> TO <end> [STEP <step>]
 [statements]
 [EXIT FOR]
 [statements]
NEXT [counter]
```

The **<step>** argument can be either positive or negative. The value of the step argument determines loop processing as follows:

Once the loop starts and all statements in the loop have executed, **<step>** is added to **<counter>**. At this point, either the statements in the loop execute again (based on the same test that caused the loop to execute initially), or the loop is exited and execution continues with the line following the **Next** statement.

while...wend

The **while...wend** loop executes a set of statements are long as the while condition is true. This is similar to the **do while...enddo** construct from Xbase. Its syntax is:

```
WHILE <condition>
 [statements]
WEND
```

The **<condition>** is some expression that evaluates to either true or false. As long as the condition is true, the statements inside will be performed. The loop will continue until the **<condition>** is no longer valid; however, it is only tested once per iteration. If the condition changes in the middle of the statements, the remaining statements will still be processed. Once the condition is false, the program continues at the next statement after the **WEND** statement.

Functions

Both Visual Basic and Delphi have a large number of built in functions, similar to Xbase languages. Most of the database functions, such as EOF and BOF, are methods of the data objects, while the more general purpose functions are generally available at any time, not restricted to the scope of an object. In this section, we will review some of the common Xbase functions and show their Delphi and Visual Basic counterparts.

Arithmetic Functions

All Xbase languages, Delphi, and Visual Basic provide a number of functions that allow you to perform arithmetic operations. Table 9.3 lists some of the more common arithmetic functions available in the languages.

Table 9.3 Arithmetic Functions

Xbase	Visual Basic	Delphi	Description
Abs()	Abs()	Abs()	Absolute value of a number
	Atn()	Arctan()	Arctangent of a number
	Cos()	Cos()	Cosine of an angle
Exp()	Exp()	Exp()	Returns exponential of argument
Int()	Int()	Int()	Returns integer portion of a number
Log()	Log()	Ln()	Computes natural logarithm
Round()	Fix()	Round()	Rounds a number to decimal places
Sqrt()	Sqrt()	Sqrt()	Calculates a square root of a number

Date Functions

The date functions allow you to extract pieces from dates, including the numeric day of week or month, the month number, and the year number. In addition, you can extract month or day names from date variables. Although Object Pascal does not specifically have a date data type, it does create a serial number indicating the number of days past January 1, 0001. The date functions manipulate this number as a date, even though it is actually a floating pointer number.

Table 9.4 Date Functions

Xbase	Visual Basic	Delphi	Description
Cdow()		Typed Constants	Returns character day of week
Cmonth()		Typed Constants	Returns month name
Ctod()	Cdate()	StrToDate()	Convert character to a date
Date()	Date()	Date()	Returns the current system date
Day()	Day()	DecodeDate()	Returns day number of month
Dow()	WeekDay()	DayofWeek()	Returns numeric day of week
Dtoc()	DateToStr()		Converts date to character string
Dtos()		DateToStr()	Converts date to string
Month()	Month()	DecodeDate()	Returns month number
Year()	Year()	DecodeDate()	Returns year number

Typed Constants refer to some global arrays created by Object Pascal that contain month names (**ShortMonthNames** and **LongMonthNames**) as well as days names (**ShortDayNames** and **LongDayNames**). You can use these array references by passing the proper parameter, either month number or day number.

File/Environment Functions

Both Visual Basic and Delphi have a large number of functions, probably more than Xbase languages, for querying the current environment. Table 9.5 lists a few examples of some of the functions available.

Table 9.5 File/Environment Functions

Xbase	Visual Basic	Delphi	Description
Curdir()	Curdir$()	GetDir()	Returns current directory name
Diskspace()		DiskFree()	Amount of disk space remaining
File()	GetAttr()	FileExists()	Does a file exist?

String Functions

String manipulation is as strong in both Visual Basic and Delphi as it is in Xbase languages. Table 9.6 lists a few examples of some of the functions available for manipulating string variables.

Table 9.6 String Functions

Xbase	Visual Basic	Delphi	Description
At()	Instr()	Pos()	Search for substrings within a string
Left()	Left$()	Copy()	Extract characters from left of string
Len()	Len()	Length()	Get length in chars of a string
Lower()	Lcase$()	LowerCase()	Convert string to lowercase
Right()	Right$()	Copy()	Extract characters from right of string
Str()	Str()	Str()	Converts a number to a string
Stuff()	Mid()	Insert()/Delete()	Insert/replace substrings
Substr()	Mid$()	Copy()	Extract pieces from a string
Upper()	Ucase$()	UpperCase()	Converts a string to uppercase
Val()	Val()	Val()	Converts a string to a number

Printing

Now that we've explored some of the programming language constructs in VB and Delphi, let's look at some example programming tasks that are accomplished using the language syntax rather than visually. The first task is that of printing, which Delphi and Visual Basic handle similarly by leaving the details to Windows.

The Printer Object

In Xbase, we typically use the following statements to enable printing.

```
SET PRINTER TO <destination>
SET CONSOLE OFF
SET PRINT ON

? "Print some stuff...   "
?? " Print some more stuff"

SET PRINT OFF
SET PRINTER TO
SET CONSOLE ON
```

In both Delphi and Visual Basic, the **Printer** object enables communication with a system printer (initially the default system printer) and the same functionality as the Xbase printing statements. When programs start in either language, a global variable that contains the printer object is automatically created.

In Delphi, the **Printers** unit must be specifically included, which is similar to linking a library into your application, in order to have the printer variable created. The Printer variable's methods and properties control the printing process.

Selecting Where to Print

The **Printer** variable is initially set to the default Windows printer. In Visual Basic, a global array called **Printers** exists that contains the list of all available printers.

For example, Figure 9.1 shows a printer list from Windows 95.

Figure 9.1 Windows 95 printer list.

Based on this list of printers, the **Printers** array in Visual Basic would contain the following:

```
Printers[0] = "Microsoft Fax"
Printers[1] = "FX Works"
Printers[2] = "HP Laserjet Series II"
Printers[3] = "Panasonic KX-P1124"
```

Switching the printer variable to any of the defined printers is accomplished with the **SET PRINTER** command in Visual Basic. For example, the following command would set the current printer to the HP Laserjet printer.

```
SET PRINTER = Printers(2)
```

The user can change the default printer by using the printer common dialog boxes discussed in Chapter 8 or the user can select from a list box that was loaded with the contents of the printers array.

In Delphi, the **Printers** array is a property of the printer object. To assign a specific printer from the printers array to the printer object, set the printer's **PrinterIndex** property to the integer array element. If you set **PrinterIndex** to -1, the default printer is used. You can also set up a common dialog box to allow the user to change the default printer.

Starting the Print Job

Once the printer is selected, you start output to the printer by calling the BeginDoc method. This method is similar to the **SET PRINT ON** command, in that it creates a print job to hold subsequent output. The output is buffered into a temporary file until the application closes the print job.

Adjusting Printer Properties

There are a large number of properties that impact how the print job is printed. For example, the **Orientation** property determines landscape or portrait printing, the **Pagewidth** (Delphi) / **Width** (Visual Basic) set the width of the printed page.

Although a dialog box could be created to edit these properties, you should probably call the **PrinterSetup** common dialog box and allow the user to adjust the properties. Of course, if the properties need to be adjusted for your report to run properly, you can easily do so in your application's code.

Writing to the Printer

In Delphi, once you've set the printer object up, the **Canvas** object is available for all output to that printer. You can set the font for the canvas to any valid font, as well as draw various shapes using the **Arc**, **Chord**, **Pie**, and other methods.

However, text is output using the **TextOut** method, which requires a pixel location and a text string to write. The text is then written in the current font. For example, Listing 9.1 illustrates some Delphi code to print a short text to the printer.

Listing 9.1 Printing text in Delphi.

```
begin
  Printer.BeginDoc;          { begin to send print job to printer }
  Printer.Canvas.TextOut(20,20,'Delphi is fun!');
  Printer.Canvas.TextOut(20,40,'It makes programming easier!');
  Printer.EndDoc;            { EndDoc ends and starts printing }
end;
```

Keep in mind, however, that coordinates are expression in column row order (although actually in pixels) rather than the row/column order that Xbase uses. In Visual Basic, you can use the Print method to print directly to the printer object, without the necessity of a **Canvas** object. Listing 9.2 shows similar text printed from Visual Basic.

Listing 9.2 Printing text in Visual Basic.

```
Printer.Print 'Visual Basic is fun!'
Printer.Print 'It makes Windows programming easy!'
Printer.EndDoc
```

Cancelling the Print Job

The printer object has a method called **KillDoc** in Visual Basic and **Abort** in Delphi. If you send this message to the object, the print job will be cancelled, and the printer device will proceed to the next job in the queue. You might want to respond to a click while the job is printing by asking the user if they would like to cancel the print job.

For example, the following code fragments give the user the option to cancel the current print job:

Visual Basic:

```
if MsgBox ("Cancel printing", vbYesNo, "Print job") = vbYes
 Printer.KillDoc
 Printer.EndDoc
end if
```

```
if MessageDlg ('Cancel?',mtError,[mbYes,mbNo],0) = mrYes then
printer.abort;
```

Finish Printing

The **EndDoc** method ends the current print job and closes the text file variable. After the application calls **EndDoc**, the printer should begin printing. This is similar to the **SET PRINT OFF** and **SET PRINTER TO** Xbase commands.

Error Handling

Error handling is one area of Xbase where there is very little standardization. Clipper uses error blocks while FoxPro uses the ON ERROR command. Both Delphi and Visual Basic offer good error handling methods as well. Visual Basic's on Error trapping is similar to FoxPro's (after all they are written by the same company), while the Object Pascal error handling is modeled after C++.

Visual Basic Exception Handling

Errors in Visual Basic are handled by specifying a routine to be called when an error occurs. The **ON ERROR** statement is used to specify the routine to call if an error occurs. Its syntax is:

```
ON ERROR  GOTO <Error_routine>
```

When an error is encountered, Visual Basic passes control the error handling function. An **ERR** object is created and available in the error routine to determine what happened and to decide how to resolve the error. This is similar to Clipper's **Error** object, with properties that get filled with appropriate error information. The **Number** property and the **Description** property are useful in determining the appropriate action. Often the **Description** property is shown in the text of an error message for the user to respond to.

In general, the error routine will consist of a **case** statement or a series of **if..else** statements. Once the appropriate section of code is found, the user can either stop the program execution by using the **STOP** statement. This is probably too dramatic for all errors. More likely, the **RESUME** statement would be used. Its syntax is:

RESUME [0]	Resume at the line causing the error and retry it.
RESUME NEXT	Resume at the line immediately after the error.
RESUME <label>	Resume at a particular line number /label

Listing 9.3 shows a sample Visual Basic error handling routine.

Listing 9.3 Visual Basic CheckError().

```
Function CheckError

select case err.number
case 64,52          ' Invalid file name, bad file name
 Msg = "Bad file name, try again"
case 71             ' Drive door is opened
 Msg="Shut the door, its cold in here"
case 68
 Msg="No such device"
case else
 Msg="Your guess is as good as mine"
end select
resume
```

Delphi Exception Handling

Delphi handles errors by allowing you to create protected blocks of code. A protected block of code is code that is executed sequentially, but jumps to a specific portion of the block if any error occurs. The syntax to create a protected block is:

```
try
  { statements you want to protect }
except
  { exception-handling statements }
end;
```

The application executes the statements in the **except** part only if an exception occurs during execution of the statements in the try part. Execution of the try part statements includes routines called by code in the **try** part. This is similar to the BEGIN SEQUENCE... RECOVER... END blocks in Clipper.

If the code completes without an error, the exception block is skipped. In either case, execution continues at the end of the current block.

In addition to the **except** keyword, you can also use a **finally** keyword. The difference is that exceptions will branch to the **finally** code just like the except clause. However, if the code completes with no exceptions, the **finally** code will then be executed. This is useful for times when processing should be done at the end of the routine or if an error occurs. For example, if you open a communications port within the routine, you should close the port regardless of whether or not an error occurs.

Listing 9.4 shows a sample Delphi exception routine.

Listing 9.4 Delphi exception routine.

```
function GetAverage(Sum, NumberOfItems: Integer): Integer;
begin
  try
    Result := Sum div NumberOfItems;
  except
    on EDivByZero do Result := 0;
  end;
end;
```

The Windows API

With any Xbase language, you have probably used function libraries on occasion. One of Clipper's strongest attributes is its incredible number of function libraries, since Clipper was designed early to accommodate user-defined functions. However, when you are programming in the Windows environment, you have access to one of the larger function libraries, called the Windows API.

The Windows API is a function library that gives access to all of Windows. Much of Delphi or Visual Basic code will get translated into calls to functions within the API. While a lot of this is done behind the scenes, knowing how to access the API pretty much removes all restrictions from the language. If Windows can do it, and you can figure out which functions in the API make it work, then your program can do it as well.

Accessing the API from Delphi

To access Windows API functions directly from within Delphi, include the WinProcs and WinTypes units in the code that will access the API. This sets up the function calls and special Windows data types for interfacing with the API.

Accessing the API from Visual Basic

Accessing the Windows API from Visual Basic requires a bit more work than from Delphi. The Visual Basic DECLARE statement must be used to declare references to external procedures in the dynamic-link libraries (DLL) used by Windows. The syntax is:

```
Declare Function name Lib "libname"  [([args])][As type]
```

Basically, to access the API you need to declare the function name and which DLL it can be found. Fortunately, Visual Basic includes text files that contain all the standard function declarations and data types. These text files can be read and the needed API function calls cut and pasted into your application.

Summary

While the visual design tools are one of the first things you notice about Delphi and Visual Basic, you can see that the language behind the scenes is powerful. Both languages have matured over the years to the point where you can write reliable and efficient code in either language. Visual Basic is closer to Xbase because it is also based upon an interpretive language, so the rules and structure are a little less stringent. Object Pascal is a native code compiler, which has stricter rules, but produces a single EXE file rather than relying upon any DLL files. Whichever language you choose, you can't go wrong. Both will take getting used to, particularly after working in Xbase, however, both will allow you to quickly write Windows programs.

CHAPTER 10:

WRITING YOUR SECOND WINDOWS PROGRAM

Chapter 1 looked at a simple list of tasks and the corresponding menu structure. The following chapters looked at building the menu system and how to attach code to the various menu options. This chapter looks at the potential steps used to develop the same system under Windows (or any GUI-based, object oriented system).

What Exactly We are Trying to Accomplish

Xbase languages have brought programming to a wider audience than the more formal C or COBOL languages. The design and syntax of Xbase languages allow for more rapid development of database systems than traditional programming languages. One down side, however, is that often people dive right into programming, without the benefit of a formal design. It is often hard to explain why a proper design often takes longer than the actual programming to implement it.

Unfortunately, Visual Basic and Delphi unintentionally contribute to this program—first, design-as-you-go approach, which I call **ready...fire...aim**. Both Visual Basic and Delphi make it very easy to program screens and controls with very little thought to the design behind it. Regardless of the language used, a good design is essential to produce a reliable and useful application.

Start with the System Turned Off

The first step of an application design should be done with the computer turned off!

As intuitive as it may seem, many people forget that the first step is to decide what you want the program to do. I also would encourage you to take the time to write it down. And refer back to this goal as you get further into your programming efforts. Try to see how each task you program contributes towards the goal of the system.

Looking back at our accounting system from Chapter 1, we could say that our goal is:

To record various transactions in the appropriate journals and ledgers to allow us to produce standard reports to measure the financial status of the company.

By having a goal, each task can be measured to see if it contributes to the overall purpose of the system. Too often, it is tempting to add neat features to the application, which don't directly contribute to the goal. It is easy to create a system that, although it has so many incredible features, no one wants to use it. Keep the goal in mind at all times, and place it in front of you when you turn the computer on.

Creating the Task List

Once the system goal has been defined, come up with a list of tasks that the user typically performs in order to accomplish the goal. The task list could be short and direct, or a complex undertaking with many subtasks. The task list should try to determine the most important tasks that need to be implemented in your application.

Accounting System Task List

After meeting with the users of the accounting system we are trying to model, we have come up with the following tasks:

Create/Edit Account Numbers

This task concerns creating categories, called account numbers, for each group of transaction we are concerned with. The user needs to be able to edit the categories, create new ones, and removed unused ones. Because these categories will be used to provide detail on our financial statements, this task seems directly related to our overall goal.

Record Journal Entries

Recording account numbers, dates, transaction amounts, and so on in a standard double-entry bookkeeping manner. These journal entries may be put in one journal or grouped into subsidiary journals, primarily depending upon the volume of transactions.

Post Journal Entries

Rather than apply the journal entries directly against the ledger, this periodic process records all unapplied transactions against appropriate ledger accounts and flags the transactions as posted.

Monthly Closing

Each month (or some other period), the transactions in temporary accounts (i.e. revenues and expenses) are summed up and transferred into permanent accounts (assets, liabilities, and equity). This process is known as closing, and generally is done a few days after the end of the period to provide time for all transactions to be recorded.

Write Checks

Since cash is the lifeblood of most businesses, tracking it is essential to measuring the financial status of the business. Writing checks entails both printing the check and deducting the check amount from the cash balance. This is a specialized journal entry that will need to be recorded against the ledger.

Pay Bills

Most business will receive bills for services and products. The bills need to be recorded to track which vendors to send payment when the check is written, and more importantly, to mark the bill as paid.

Post Deposits

If we only write checks all day long, the business won't last very long. We probably want to make sure that money is posted into the account. As a matter of fact, lets make sure the system strongly encourages such transactions.

Add/Edit Customers

The customers are the people we hope to provide goods or offer services to, in exchange for monetary gain. We need to keep track of the customers, although the actual demographic information will not appear anywhere on our financial statements. Instead, customers are ancillary, but necessary to the process of recording deposits.

Create/Edit Invoices

The customers are not likely to pay if payment isn't requested. It is necessary that the system can produce invoices on demand to send to customers.

Apply Payments to Invoices

As each customer pays us, we need to apply the payments to the proper invoices. This allows us to keep track of all outstanding invoices, as well as possibly monitoring customer orders for future trends and to provide input to the marketing cycle.

Print Financial Reports

This is the ultimate goal of the system, to produce financial reports. These include a balance sheet, an income statement, and a statement of changes in financial position.

We will probably want to be able to produce each statement for the current period and any prior period.

Finding the Objects

If you recall from chapter one, we immediately grouped our tasks into a menu structure (See Listing 10.1) However, when designing a system for an object based platform, such as Windows, the menu is not the next step, nor even a necessary step.

Listing 10.1 Menu structure to navigate task list.

```
General Ledger
 Chart of Accounts
 Journal Entries
 Post Entries
 Close the Books
 Financial Reporting
   Balance Sheet
   Income Statement
   Statement of Changes in Financial Position
Checkbook
 Check Register
 Pay Bills
 Print Checks
 Make Deposits
 Bank Reconciliation
Accounts Receivable/Invoicing
 Customer File maintenance
 Invoicing for Services
 Applying Payments
 Past due Processing
 Printing Invoices
```

Rather than using an arbitrary menu structure to group our tasks, a different approach is to look for the objects or entities that are represented in the task list. A simple first approach is to isolate all of the nouns from the task to see which are objects. The verbs in the list represent the actions that must be applied to those objects. Table 10.1 shows such a breakdown.

Table 10.1 Objects and Tasks

Objects	Tasks
Ledger/books/accounts	Create/edit
	Close
Journals	Record entries
	Post
Checkbook	Write Checks
	Print Checks
	Make Deposits
Bills	Record Bills
	Mark bills as paid
Customers	Create/edit
Invoices	Create/edit
	Apply payments to
	Print

The tasks are now organized by objects, rather than a menu structure. The user-interface may seem more familiar to the end-user, rather than requiring the user to navigate a menu structure.

Reviewing the objects and tasks is a recursive process. Once the system is broken down into objects and tasks applied to those object, review the system with the users. Often, just breaking the objects out will cause the user to think of more tasks. For example, in our menu structure, we included an option called *Bank Reconciliation* and another called *Past Due Processing*. Both of these tasks should be added to the list of tasks, Bank Reconciliation attached to the checkbook object and Past Due Processing attached to the customer object. In addition, we probably should add the reports and tasks that must be done to product the reports. Table 10.2 shows the final object/task table, with the additions.

Table 10.2 Final Object/Task Table

Objects	Tasks
Ledger/books/accounts	Create/edit
	Close
	Print accounts and trial balance
Journals	Record entries
	Post
	Print journal entries
	Reverse journal entries
	Search journals
Checkbook	Write Checks
	Print Checks
	Make Deposits
	Bank reconciliation
	Service and other miscellaneous charges
Customers	Create/edit
	Past Due Processing
	Statements and letters
	Print customer lists
Invoices	Create/edit
	Apply payments to
	Print
	Issue credits against invoices
Reports	Select reporting period
	Print standard reports
	Custom reports

In addition to the user objects, some tasks that don't have any objects are needed. For example, packing and reindexing the files is a new task the system should provide, although there is probably no counterpart in the manual system.

Designing the Data Structures

After the objects and tasks have been determined, the data structures that will represent all of the data within the objects must be designed. In this step, consider each object and list the fields that need to keep track of. Also consider our primary and secondary keys, as well as relationships. This process, called *normalization*, is a standard step regardless of the target platform. Even in a DOS application, normalization of your databases should be done before coding starts.

Normalization—A Brief Review

Database normalization is an attempt to reduce redundant data and produce a more streamlined file system. Each object in your design will probably be represented in at least one logical file. A logical file is a group of information that needs to be tracked for that object. The normalization process will break that logical file into a number of physical tables (in our case DBF files) that allow the computer to record the information in the logical file in a consistent, reliable manner.

A complete discussion of normalization is beyond the scope of this book, although it is also something that many times is done intuitively. Even if you have never *normalized* a set of files, you might find yourself saying, "Well of course, that's common sense." While a lot of normalization theory is common sense, it is nice to know that there is solid theory behind what is being done. If you want to learn more about normalization, look for the works of Codd and Date, who have written the book on normalization. However, for now, a brief review should suffice.

Place Repeating Fields into Separate Files

All repeating groups should be placed into a separate table or tables. For example, in our invoice object, we probably have a logical file as shown in Table 10.3.

Table 10.3 Logical Invoice File

customer_id	
invoice_number	
sales_rep	
salesman_name	
order_date	
quantity	These fields are repeated for each item on the invoice, could be anywhere from one to hundreds of items.
part_number	
price	

This logical invoice file should be broken into at least two files. One file will contain the heading invoice, customer id, sales_rep, etc., and the second file will contain the invoice that repeats, quantity, part_number, and price. These files will need to be linked together by selecting some sort of key field, in this case the invoice-number.

Table 10.4 shows the logical invoice file broken into two tables.

Table 10.4 Invoice File with Repeating Information Removed

Table Inv_hdr	Table Inv_det
Customer_id	Invoice_number
Invoice_number	Part_number
Sales_rep	Quantity
Salesman_name	Price
Order_date	

To represent the logical invoice file, you would have at least one entry in the **Inv_hdr** table and any number of entries in the **Inv_det** table. To determine which items belong with which invoices, would link them together via the ***Invoice_number*** field, which is common to both files. If you look at an actual invoice, shown in Figure 10.1, the same breakdown between the header section and multiple line items can be seen.

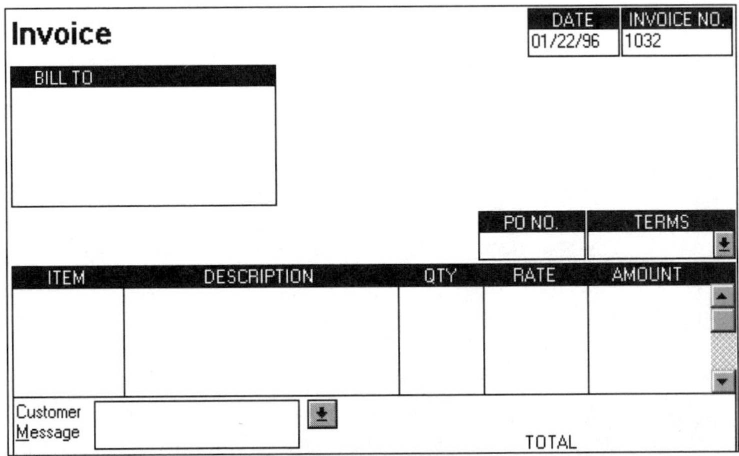

Figure 10.1 Typical paper invoice.

In breaking the file apart, we need to duplicate the invoice number between the two files. In the Inv_det table, Invoice_number is known as a foreign key and is used to link the two files together. A foreign key is linked to a primary key in another database. A primary key is a unique identifier for every database and is essential for good database design that all records in the file can be uniquely identified.

Remove Nondependent Data into Separate Files

Once repeating groups are removed into separate tables, review the data tables for nondependent data. Non-dependent data is data that is not solely dependent upon the primary key of the file. For example, in our Inv_hdr file, the salesman_name is not dependent upon the invoice_number, but rather is dependent upon the sales_rep initials. Rather than repeat the salesman_name in every invoice, we should extract the salesman_name into a separate file keyed by sales_rep. Table 10.5 illustrates the modified table structure.

Table 10.5 Invoice File Without Non-Dependent Data

Inv_hdr	Inv_det
Customer_id	Invoice_number
Invoice_number	Part_number
Sales_rep	Quantity
Order_date	Price

Salesman table

Sales_rep

Salesman_name

You might also consider **price** to be nondependent (unless separate prices are charged to different customers). This is because the **part_number** should be used to determine price, not the invoice number. If this were the case, you might add the following table, while removing price from the Inv_det table.

Part File

Part_number

Price

As an Xbase programmer, you have probably normalized tables (even though you might not have know the name for what you were doing). However, if this is new to you, take the time to research normalization because it is one of the best ways to produce solid database designs.

Indexing Caveat

When planning your databases in Visual Basic or Delphi, be very careful of your indexing expressions. In Xbase, the index can be an expression that might not exist directly in any database field, but rather is derived through a function call. A good example would be the **soundex** function to order your database by phonetic spelling. While this is a powerful feature of Xbase, many SQL systems key on the columns (fields) in the database, rather than expressions. Try to keep index expressions to simple column definitions, which will make it easier to scale the program to a client server environment. If a function is needed as an index key, consider adding a field and populating the field with the function value. This will allow indexing on that field directly, which SQL systems will be able to work with.

Designing the Objects

At this point, you have found all the component pieces, the objects, the tasks, and the databases. The next step, and arguably the most fun, is to design the screens and write the code that will make the objects work. This is where the visual tools come into play.

Ledger Object

As an example, let's consider the **Ledger** object, which is basically a list of account numbers with descriptions and balances attached to it. The tasks consist of editing the account, closing a period, and printing the accounts. Figure 10.2 shows a possible screen for the **Ledger** object.

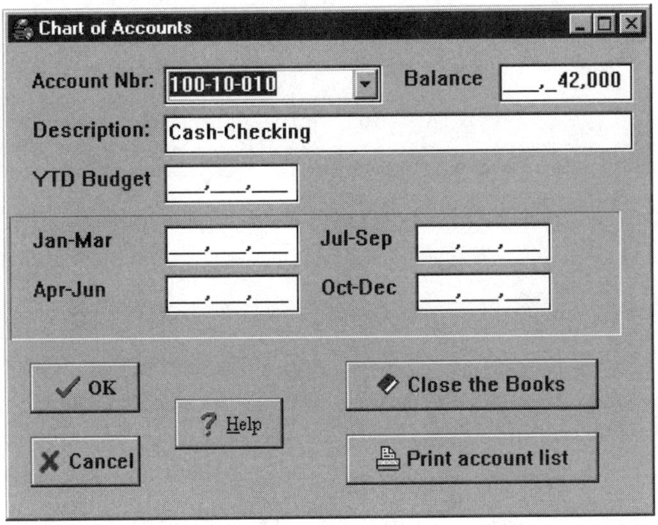

Figure 10.2 Ledger object.

Although we could have more fun designing this screen, it provides the functionality necessary to manipulate the object according to the tasks described.

Bills Object

To illustrate another object, lets take a look at the **Bills** object from QuickBooks. QuickBooks from Intuit is a good example of an object based accounting system, which consist of invoices, bills, and checks. If you are designing any kind of financial system, get a copy of QuickBooks. Not only does it keep track of your money, but it illustrates a lot of good object based design principles.

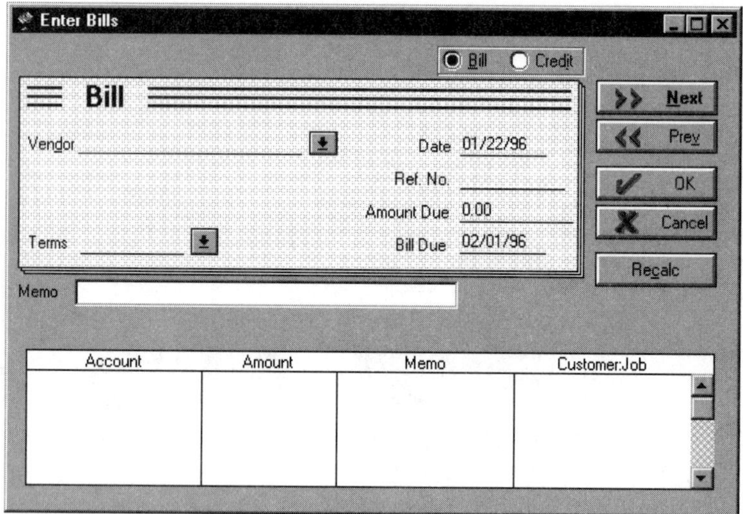

Figure 10.3 The bill object from QuickBooks.

Now What?

Once you've designed all your objects, the next question is how are they presented to the user? A menu is one approach, and certainly has merit if your users are coming from a DOS platform. Another approach is to design icon images placed together in a group which the user can choose from. Selecting the appropriate image brings up the select object for editing. Figure 10.4 shows the toolbar from QuickBooks.

Figure 10.4 QuickBook toolbar.

Work with the users and review similar applications to determine the best method of presenting your design. After all, the hard work is done, now the fun of letting the user work with it begins.

Summary

Windows programming is different from DOS programming, but with tools like Visual Basic and Delphi, it is no longer the exclusive realm of the C or C++ coders.

By this point, you should have the confidence to grab a massive book about Visual Basic or Delphi and dig in. However, be forewarned; once you dig in, you will find so many new techniques to apply to help you write your applications, that it will be hard to turn back to DOS. Good luck!

APPENDIX A:

XBASE, DELPHI, AND VISUAL BASIC EQUIVALENTS

This appendix lists some of the common commands and functions from Xbase and shows their Delphi and Visual Basic counterparts. Note that the Xbase column contains commands and functions from all versions of Xbase, not just one dialect.

Xbase	Delphi	Visual Basic
% OPERATOR	MOD operator	MOD operator
$ OPERATOR	Pos() function	Instr() function
@ .. BOX	tPANEL, tBEVEL component	Shape control
@ .. EDIT	tMEMO component	Edit control, with multiline property set to TRUE
@ .. GET	tEDIT component	Edit control
@ .. GET CHECK		
@ .. GET PICTURE '@*C"	tCHECKBOX component	Checkbox control
@ .. GET LIST,		
@ .. GET FROM/POPUP	tLISTBOX component	Listbox control
@ .. GET PUSHBUTTON		
@ .. GET PICTURE '@*'	tBUTTON component	CommandButton control
@ .. GET RADIO		
@ .. GET PICTURE '@*R'	tRADIOGROUP component	OptionButtons control
@ .. GET SPINNER	tSPINBUTTON component	Spin button control
@ .. PROMPT	tMENUITEM component	MenuItem control
@.. SAY	tLABEL component	Label control
@.. SAY BITMAP	tIMAGE component	Image control
@..TO	tPANEL,tBEVEL component	Shape control
ABS()	Abs() function	Abs() function

ACHOICE()	tLISTBOX component	Listbox control
AFIELDS()	tTABLE.FieldDefs property	RecordSet.Fields collection
ALERT()	MessageBox() function	MsgBox() function
ALIAS()	tTABLE.DataBaseName property	Database name property
APPEND BLANK	tTABLE.Append, tTABLE.AppendRecord	RecordSet.AddNew Method
APPEND FROM	tTABLE.BatchMove	INSERT SQL Statement
ASC()	Ord() function	Asc() function
AT()	Pos() function	Instr() function
ATAN()	ArcTan() function	Atn() function
BEGIN SEQUENCE	try..except..end statements	
BOF()	tTABLE.Bof() property	RecordSet.Bof() property
BROWSE	tDBGrid Component	dbGrid() component
CDOW()	Typed constants	Format() function
CHR()	Chr() function	Chr() function
CMONTH()	Typed Constants	Format() function
COMMIT	tTABLE.Post	RecordSet.Update method
COPY TO	tTABLE.BatchMove() method	RecordSet.GetRows() method
COS()	Cos() function	Cos() function
CREATE	tTABLE.CreateTable() method	Database.CreateTableDef() method
CTOD()	StrToDate() function	DateValue() function
CURDIR()	GetDir()	CurDir$() function
DATE()	Date() function	Date() function
DAY()	DecodeDate() function	Day() function
DBF()	tTABLE.Databasename propery	Database name property
DBSTRUCT()	tTABLE.FieldDefs property	Database.TableDefs collection
DELETE	tTABLE.Delete() method	RecordSet.Delete method
DELETE FILE	DeleteFile() function	Kill statement
DELETE TAG	tTABLE.Deleteindex() method	Index.Delete() method
DISKSPACE()	DiskFree() function	

DO CASE	case ...else... end statements	Select case...case...end select
DO WHILE	while...do and repeat...until	do while|until ... enddo
DOW()	DayofWeek() function	WeekDay() function
DTOC()	DateToStr() function	Cdate() function
EJECT	tPRINTER.NewPage() method	PRINTER.NewPage() method
EOF()	tTABLE.Eof() property	RecordSet.Eof() property
EXP()	Exp() function	Exp() function
FCLOSE()	FileClose() function	Close statement
FCOUNT()	tTABLE.FieldCount() property	Recordset.Recordcount property
FCREATE()	FileCreate() function	Open for output statement
FGETS()	FileRead() function	GET # statement
FILE()	FileExists() function	GetAttr() function
FLUSH	tTABLE.Post() method	RecordSet.Update method
FOPEN()	FileOpen() function	Open for input statement
FOR...NEXT	for...next do statements	for...endfor|next statements
FPUTS()	FileWrite() function	Put # statement
FREAD()	FileRead() function	Get # statement
FSEEK()	FileExist() function	Seek # statement
FWRITE()	FileWrite() function	Put # statement
GO / GOTO	tTABLE.GoToBookMark	RecordSet.Bookmark property
GO BOTTOM	tTABLE.Last method	RecordSet.MoveLast method
GO TOP	tTABLE.First method	RecordSet.MoveFirst method
IF...ENDIF	if...end statements	if..then...else statements
INSERT	tTABLE.Insert method	INSERT INTO SQL statement
INDEX	tTABLE.AddIndex method	TableDef.CreateIndex method
INT()	Int() function	Int() function
LASTREC()	tTABLE.RecordCount() property	Recordset.Recordcount property

LEFT()	Copy() function	Left$() function
LEN()	Length() function	Len() function
LOG()	Ln() function	Log() function
LOWER()	Lowercase() function	Lcase$() function
MAX()	Max() function	Max() function
MEMOEDIT()	tMEMO Component	Edit control, with multiline property set to TRUE
MENU TO	tMAINMENU component	MENU Component
MIN()	Min() function	Min() function
MOD()	Mod operator	Mod operator
MONTH()	DecodeDate() function	Month() function
ORDER()	tTABLE.Indexname property	TABLEDEF.Index name property
ORDKEY()	tTABLE.IndexFieldnames property	TABLEDEF.Index fields collection
ORDNAME()	tTABLE.Indexname property	TABLEDEF.Index name property
ORDSCOPE()	tTABLE.SetRange method	SQL select statement
QUIT	tFORM.Close() method	END statement
RDDNAME()	tTABLE.TableType property	Database.Version property
RECCOUNT()	tTABLE.RecordCount property	Recordset.Recordcount property
RECNO()	tTABLE.Bookmark property	RecordSet.Bookmark property
RENAME	Rename() procedure	NAME statement
REPLICATE()	Concat() function	String() function
RIGHT()	Copy() function	Right$() function
ROUND()	Round() function	cInt() function
RUN	WinExec() function	Shell() function
SECONDS()	Now() function	Now() function
SEEK	tTABLE.FindKey() method	Database.Seek method

SET CURSOR	tFORM.Cursor Property	MousePointer property
SET EXCLUSIVE	tTABLE.Exclusive property	Data.Exclusive property
SET INDEX TO	tTABLE.Indexname property	RecordSet.Indexname property
SET ORDER TO	tTABLE.Indexname property	RecordSet.Indexname property
SET PRINT OFF	tPRINTER.Begindoc() method	PRINTER.BeginDoc()
SET PRINT ON	tPRINTER.Enddoc() method	PRINTER.EndDoc()
SET PRINTER TO	tPRINTER.PrinterIndex property,	SET PRINTER = Printer(number)
SET RELATION	tTABLE.Mastersource and MasterFields properties	Database.CreateRelation method
SET SCOPE	tTABLE.Setrange() method	SQL select statement
SKIP +1	tTABLE.Next() method	RecordSet.MoveNext method
SKIP -1	tTABLE.Prior() method	RecordSet.MovePrevious method
SKIP +/- <n>	tTABLE.MoveBy() method	RecordSet.Move method
SQRT()	Sqrt() function	Sqr() function
STR()	Str() function	Str() function
SUBSTR()	Copy() function	Mid$() function
TIME()	Time() function	Time statement
TRANSFORM()	FmtStr() function	Format() function
UPPER()	Uppercase() function	Ucase$() function
USE	tTABLE.Open() method or tTABLE.Active property	OpenRecordSet method DataBase Object.
USED()	tTABLE.Active property	
VAL()	Val() Function	Val() function
YEAR()	DecodeDate() function	Year() function
ZAP	tTABLE.EmptyTable() method	SQL Delete statement

INDEX

E

F

G

H

S

T

U

V

W

X

Y

Z